SKY WAS NEVER THE LIMIT

SKY WAS NEVER THE LIMIT

The Story of
Shubhanshu Shukla

Narayan R.

Published by
Rupa Publications India Pvt. Ltd 2025
161-B/4, Gulmohar House,
Yusuf Sarai Community Centre,
New Delhi 110049

Sales centres:
Bengaluru Chennai
Hyderabad Kolkata Mumbai

Copyright © Rupa Publications India Pvt. Ltd 2025

The views and opinions expressed in this book are the author's own and the facts are as reported by him; these have been verified to the extent possible, and the publishers are not in any way liable for the same.

All rights reserved.
No part of this publication may be reproduced, transmitted, or stored in a retrieval system, in any form or by any means, electronic, mechanical, photocopying, recording or otherwise, without the prior permission of the publisher.

P-ISBN: 978-93-7003-802-8
E-ISBN: 978-93-7003-521-8

First impression 2025

10 9 8 7 6 5 4 3 2 1

The moral right of the author has been asserted.

Printed in India

This book is sold subject to the condition that it shall not, by way of trade or otherwise, be lent, resold, hired out or otherwise circulated, without the publisher's prior consent, in any form of binding or cover other than that in which it is published.

Contents

Prologue — *vii*

1. From Lucknow to the Stars: Early Life of Astronaut Shubhanshu Shukla — 1

2. From Cadet to Combat Pilot — 20

3. Becoming Gaganyatri: The Astronaut Transformation — 45

4. Touching the Heavens—Launch, Docking and Life Aboard ISS — 69

5. Experiments in the Cosmic Lab — 78

6. Homecoming—Return to Earth and a Hero's Welcome — 111

7. Building the Bridge to Gaganyaan: Legacy, Leadership and the Next Generation — 139

Sources — 143

Prologue

He was not born among rockets or runways, but beneath open skies where stars whispered secrets to the sleepless.

In the hushed corners of Lucknow, a boy once dreamed of touching the heavens—not with noise, but with knowing. **Shubhanshu Shukla**, quiet-eyed and resolute, chased constellations with mathematics, mapped flightpaths through textbooks, and held fast to the belief that even the most distant light could be reached.

Four decades after India's first spacefarer, he soared beyond Earth's cradle to the International Space Station (ISS)—**becoming the second Indian in space**, and the first to cross that threshold in a new era. This is not just the chronicle of a mission, but the odyssey of a mind—how a boy of gravity became a man of sky, and how one life rose to carry the dreams of a billion.

1
From Lucknow to the Stars: Early Life of Astronaut Shubhanshu Shukla

On a quiet October morning in 1985, in the bustling lanes of Lucknow, a boy was born into a modest home—one that had no signs of destiny written on its doors, no medals on its walls, no dreams of the sky hung above. Shubhanshu Shukla was the youngest of three children in a middle-class Hindu family, where values mattered more than wealth, and books were treasured more than toys. His father, Shambhu Dayal Shukla, a government officer with a stern sense of duty, and his mother, Asha, a gentle homemaker, nurtured their children with discipline and quiet affection. The family had no lineage of fliers or warriors, no tales of cockpits or space capsules—yet, somewhere in that simple household, a spark was taking shape.

Shubhanshu was not the kind of child who demanded attention. He didn't race through the gullies chasing kites or cricket balls. Instead, he lingered in corners with books larger than himself, tracing the stars with his fingers and filling the silence with imagination. 'He never gave us trouble,' his mother recalls, her voice tinged with wonder. 'Always with his books... he hardly stepped out to play.' His father adds, 'He had a quiet strength, a calming presence. Even as a child, he carried an unusual stillness—like he belonged to a bigger sky.'

That stillness, that curiosity, would one day propel him far beyond the streets of Lucknow—to the very edge of Earth's atmosphere, where dreams become orbit. But back then, he was simply a boy—serious, serene and silent—carrying galaxies in his mind.

'Jinhe Dekh Kar Lucknow Yaad Aaaye
Wo Adab Ki Misaal Hote Hain'

('Those who remind you of Lucknow at a glance,
are embodiments of grace and culture...')

Growing up in Lucknow—the timeless 'City of Nawabs', where *tehzeeb* meets tradition and the air hums with poetry and purpose—Shubhanshu Shukla was shaped by more than just streets and schools. He was cradled in a city that spoke in couplets, walked with grace and taught its children that knowledge was not a burden but a badge of honour. Amid the scent of kebabs, the echoes of ghazals and the quiet ambition of middle-class homes, Shukla began his journey—not with fanfare, but with fierce focus.

He attended City Montessori School (CMS), Aliganj campus—an institution as grand in its vision as the city itself. Known for nurturing global citizens with local roots, CMS had earned a UNESCO Prize for Peace Education, and it was here, amidst a sea of thousands, that a quiet boy stood out—not by voice, but by brilliance. He was the kind who listened more than he spoke, but when he did, there was precision in thought and purpose in tone. Teachers admired his discipline; classmates recall a silent force—shy but resolute.

Even Kamna, his future wife and classmate since childhood, remembers him as 'the quiet one with a never-say-never glint in his eyes'—the boy who solved problems with ease and smiled like he was carrying a secret plan. In truth, he was. The foundation of his greatness—humility, intellect and sheer determination—was already being laid, brick by brick, in the by-lanes of Lucknow. And even the city, with its fading havelis and eternal charm, seemed to whisper: *this one will rise beyond us.*

Sparks of Inspiration: Patriotism and Love for Flight

Despite having no family background in flying, Shubhanshu Shukla's childhood imagination was ignited by two key experiences that set his sights on the skies and beyond:

- **The Kargil War (1999)**: As an early teenager, Shukla was deeply inspired by the heroism of the Indian Armed Forces during the Kargil conflict. Watching news coverage of Indian soldiers and fighter pilots in action left a profound impression on him. The war's display of patriotism and bravery stirred Shubhanshu's own sense of duty. He began voicing a desire to serve the nation in uniform, telling his family that he wanted to join the armed forces to protect his country. This patriotic fire kindled by Kargil would strongly influence his career path in the years to come.
- **An Airshow's Thrill**: Around the same time, a childhood trip to an Indian Air Force airshow proved transformative for Shukla. Seeing fighter jets roar across the sky in person—the deafening thunder of engines and blur of supersonic speed—left the young boy awestruck. He was mesmerized by the speed and sound of the aircraft, according to his elder sister's recollection. It was at this airshow that Shubhanshu first voiced his dream of becoming a pilot one day. The experience planted a seed of ambition—he wanted to not just watch aeroplanes, but also fly them. From that moment, aviation became his passion. He would excitedly follow any news of aircraft and space missions, dreaming that he too might soar among the clouds or even the stars.

These early inspirations set Shukla apart from his peers. While many of his classmates were drawn to conventional career goals, young Shubhanshu's head was already in the clouds—quite literally. By his mid-teens, he had resolved to pursue a path in the Indian Air Force (IAF), which he saw as the gateway to both serving his country and quenching his thirst for flight. In the late 1990s and early 2000s, with the memory of India's only astronaut Rakesh Sharma and the resurgence of the Indian space programme on the horizon, Shukla's aspirations quietly expanded from flying fighter jets to perhaps one day venturing into space. Those ambitions, however, were kept mostly to himself—nurtured in silence until opportunity knocked.

A Secret Leap: Sneaking Out for the NDA Exam

Shubhanshu Shukla's determination to join the armed forces culminated in a dramatic turning point when he was in high school. In 2001, at just 16 years old, he made a bold move—he secretly went to take the entrance exam for the National Defence Academy (NDA) without informing his family. The NDA is India's elite joint services training academy, and admission is highly competitive, requiring candidates to pass a nationwide exam conducted by the UPSC. Shukla was still months away from finishing school, but his resolve was firm. The exam date, however, fell on an inopportune occasion—the day of his elder sister's *vidaai* (farewell ceremony) after her wedding.

On the morning of 11 December 2001, as relatives gathered and emotional rituals were underway at home, young Shubhanshu was nowhere to be found. Family members noticed his absence at the crucial moment and grew frantic—his father, Shambhu Dayal, was furious that his teenage son would disappear during such an important family event. 'Where is he? He should be here,' his worried family exclaimed while searching for him. Unbeknownst to them, Shubhanshu had quietly slipped away at dawn, cycling off to an exam centre to sit for the NDA entrance test.

Shukla had kept his plan utterly secret. In fact, he hadn't even purchased the application form himself—a close friend, who was slightly older but ineligible due to age, had obtained the NDA exam form and passed it to Shubhanshu, encouraging him to try his luck. Such was Shukla's resolve that he did not seek any help or permission; he went alone to take the exam, determined not to miss this chance. Later that day, as the family fretted, Shubhanshu casually reappeared at home 'speeding on his bicycle,' just as the ceremonies were wrapping up. 'I am here, now tell me what to do,' he said calmly, as if nothing unusual had happened.

When the truth emerged that he had left to attend the NDA exam, his relatives were astonished. The entire family was initially furious—disappearing during his sister's wedding festivities was a serious breach of expectations. But Shubhanshu did not lose his calm even under the onslaught of questions. Only a few days later did they learn the full story: he had not only *taken* the exam, he had passed it with flying colours. In fact, Shukla cleared the written test, the rigorous Services Selection Board (SSB) interviews, and the medical evaluations *all* on his own, without any guidance or fanfare. 'One day he came and told us he had cleared everything—written, SSB, medical. That's how he has always been—silently determined,' his father recalls of that moment, half proud and half amazed.

This secret NDA application became legendary in the Shukla household. What began as a rebellious gamble turned into Shubhanshu's first major triumph. His family's anger melted into pride; even his father, who had been upset at first, chose not to stand in his son's way after seeing his dedication. At 16, Shubhanshu Shukla earned admission to the National Defence Academy—setting him on the course he had dreamt about since the Kargil days. In retrospect, his family recognized this incident as a defining display of Shubhanshu's character—bold, independent, and unwavering in pursuit of his goals. His eldest sister later laughed that she hadn't even realized he was missing during the vidaai—such was Shubhanshu's quiet way of doing extraordinary things without seeking attention. The young man's 'quiet grit' in that moment, as one article noted, would come to define him.

With the NDA exam cleared and his family's blessing secured, Shukla prepared to leave the comforts of home for a life of disciplined training. The teenager from Lucknow was on the verge of transforming into a gentleman cadet at India's premier military academy.

Life at the National Defence Academy

In mid-2002, Shubhanshu Shukla entered the sprawling campus of the National Defence Academy in Khadakwasla, near Pune. Just a year earlier, he had been a high-schooler sneaking off to exams; now he donned the cadet uniform, standing shoulder to shoulder with some of the country's brightest young aspirants to military leadership. At NDA, Shukla embarked on three years of intensive education and training, an experience that would shape his physical endurance, intellect and character in equal measure. The Academy's regimen is famously tough—5.00 a.m. reveille, drill practice, long marches, academic classes and sports—but Shukla embraced it wholeheartedly. The discipline and patriotism instilled at NDA were a natural fit for the motivated youth from Lucknow who had already proven his tenacity.

Academically, Shubhanshu chose an unusual path for a future fighter pilot—he pursued a BSc degree in Computer Science at NDA. He graduated from the Academy in 2005 with this degree, having successfully balanced demanding military training with university-level studies. His focus on computer science was somewhat unique—many cadets opt for more common subjects—but it underscored Shukla's intellectual curiosity and technical bent of mind. As one account noted, this was a 'unique academic route for someone bound for space,' blending computational skills with combat training. The analytical thinking from his science education would later prove valuable in understanding complex aerospace systems.

Beyond the classroom, NDA groomed Shukla in leadership and camaraderie. He underwent army, navy and air force training modules, preparing for the day he would select his service branch. Unsurprisingly, when the time came, Shubhanshu opted for the Indian Air Force—the realization of the dream ignited by that childhood airshow. Upon passing out of NDA in late 2005, Cadet Shukla was commissioned for further training as an Air Force officer. The NDA had inculcated in him qualities of duty, discipline and devotion to the nation—values he already held dear, now reinforced by formal military ethos. It also built his confidence—the shy schoolboy from Lucknow had grown into a capable young leader of cadets. An instructor at NDA would later recall Shukla as exceptionally earnest and hardworking, someone who approached every task with methodical dedication—whether it was polishing his boots to a mirror shine or acing an advanced calculus exam.

For Shukla, graduating from NDA was a milestone—but it was not a moment of rest. It was the springboard to the next phase of his journey—learning to fly. He left NDA with a President's commission as an officer-in-training, and headed straight to the Indian Air Force Academy to earn his wings as a combat pilot.

Earning His Wings: Air Force Training and Early Career

After NDA, Shubhanshu Shukla underwent flying training at the Air Force Academy (AFA) in Dundigal, Telangana. Here, over the course of a year, he learned the fundamentals of military aviation—from basic propeller aircraft to jet trainers. Shukla's lifelong passion for flying was finally being realized in the cockpit. In June 2006, he was formally commissioned as a Flying Officer into the fighter stream of the Indian Air Force. The date marked the culmination of his boyhood dream—at 20 years old, Shukla had become a fighter pilot in the IAF. He was now Flight Lieutenant Shubhanshu Shukla, ready to serve and soar.

Over the next several years, Shukla proved himself an exceptional aviator. He mastered one aircraft after another as he moved through postings and promotions. He initially flew advanced jet trainers like the BAE Hawk to hone his skills, and soon progressed to front-line combat aircraft. Shukla had a keen aptitude for flying;

colleagues noted his ability to remain calm and make split-second decisions even under high-stress situations—traits likely rooted in the composed, focused demeanour he'd shown since youth. In the squadron, he earned the call sign 'Shux', a friendly moniker derived from his name that also reflected his easygoing yet unflappable personality.

One of the pivotal developments in Shukla's early Air Force career was his selection for the Tactics and Combat Development Establishment (TACDE)—an elite training programme often dubbed India's 'Top Gun' school. TACDE trains the top 1% of IAF pilots in advanced aerial combat tactics, teaching them to be instructors and leaders in air warfare. Shukla underwent the prestigious Fighter Combat Leader (FCL) course at TACDE, emerging as one of the 'best of the best' in the IAF. The FCL course is gruelling, but it polished Shukla's skills to a razorsharp edge. By completing it, he joined the ranks of India's elite fighter pilots qualified to devise tactics and mentor others in air combat. 'When he decides to do something, he puts in all his hard work and dedication,' his father had observed—and indeed, Shukla approached TACDE with the same quiet determination that had gotten him to NDA. Graduating as a Combat Leader burnished his credentials and confidence further.

Shukla's flying portfolio kept expanding. Over nearly two decades in service, he would log over 2,000 hours of flight time on a wide variety of aircraft. He flew supersonic fighter jets like the Sukhoi Su-30MKI (India's premier air superiority fighter), the venerable MiG-21 and modern MiG-29, as well as the Anglo-French SEPECAT Jaguar deep-strike aircraft. He also piloted strike trainers and transports such as the Hawk, the workhorse Dornier-228, and the turboprop Antonov An-32. This breadth of experience—from dogfighting at Mach 2 to low-level navigation runs—gave Shukla a well-rounded mastery of aviation technology and operations. It is a journey that very few pilots get to experience so broadly, and it speaks to Shukla's versatility and hunger to learn.

In recognition of his talent, Shubhanshu was selected to become a test pilot with the IAF's Aircraft and Systems Testing Establishment (ASTE). As a test pilot, he was responsible for evaluating new aircraft, upgrades, and weapon systems—a role requiring superior flying ability and engineering acumen. By the time he reached his late 30s, Shukla had risen to the rank of Group Captain (equivalent to a full Colonel). This promotion in March 2024 reflected his exemplary service and leadership. Within roughly 18 years, the once-rookie pilot from Lucknow had become a senior officer trusted with cutting-edge projects and the mentorship of younger pilots. Each step of the way—combat missions, tactical courses, testing experimental systems—was quietly preparing Shubhanshu Shukla for something even greater on the horizon.

Scholar of the Skies: Advanced Education and Expertise

Amid his demanding flying career, Shukla never lost the intellectual zeal that had characterized him since school. He continued to pursue higher education to deepen his understanding of aerospace engineering. In a rare accomplishment for an active-duty officer, Shubhanshu earned a master's degree in Aerospace Engineering from the Indian Institute of Science (IISc), Bengaluru. IISc is India's top research university, renowned globally for its science and engineering programmes. By undertaking an MTech there, Shukla demonstrated not only academic brilliance but also a drive to link theory with practice. Balancing military duties with graduate studies would have been challenging, but Shukla excelled—leveraging his computer science background from NDA and coupling it with advanced aerospace coursework. He likely delved into subjects like propulsion, orbital mechanics, materials, and control systems, gaining knowledge directly applicable to spacecraft and high-performance aircraft.

This advanced education fortified Shukla's technical credentials. It meant that he was not just a pilot who could fly, but also an engineer who could understand and solve complex problems in aviation and spaceflight. The dual identity of test pilot and aerospace engineer made Group Captain Shukla an ideal candidate for India's nascent human spaceflight programme. Indeed, many of history's first astronauts (from the Mercury Seven onwards) were test pilots with engineering savvy. Shukla was unknowingly following in that tradition—building the precise resume one would expect of someone bound for space—combat leadership, test flight experience, and top-tier scientific education. His profile by the mid-2010s was unique in the IAF and ISRO community, and it soon caught the attention of the country's space authorities.

Journey to the Stars: Becoming an Astronaut

In 2018–19, India's long-held ambition to launch its own crewed space mission—the Gaganyaan programme—began gathering momentum. The Indian Space Research Organisation (ISRO) set out to select and train a small group of military test pilots as potential astronauts (dubbed 'gagannauts' or gaganyatris in India). Thanks to his sterling career and skill set, Group Captain Shubhanshu Shukla was shortlisted in 2019 as one of four candidates for India's first human spaceflight team. The selection was made by the Institute of Aerospace Medicine in Bengaluru, which screened hundreds of service pilots for attributes like physical fitness, mental resilience, and technical proficiency. Shukla's quiet discipline and broad expertise made him a standout. When he got the call from ISRO in 2019, it was, as he described, 'momentous'—the opportunity to fulfill a dream that even he had scarcely imagined possible growing up.

Soon, Shukla found himself at the Yuri Gagarin Cosmonaut Training Center in Star City, Russia, embarking on a year-long astronaut training regime in early 2020. This Indo-Russian collaboration was part of a deal to prepare India's gaganyatris for space. In Star City, Shukla underwent rigorous training similar to what international astronauts receive—lessons in spacecraft systems, simulations of microgravity (including rides on parabolic 'zero-G' flights), survival training in harsh environments, space medicine courses, and learning Russian language and protocol. The training was intense and not without challenges—it demanded adapting from atmospheric flight to the nuances of orbital mechanics and life support systems. Yet Shukla thrived, completing the Russian training in 2021. A photograph from this period shows Shukla in a blue flight suit standing alongside his fellow trainees at Star City—a proud representative of India, eager to carry his nation's flag to space.

After returning from Russia, Shukla continued mission-specific training in India. ISRO established its own Astronaut Training Facility in Bengaluru where Shukla and his colleagues practised on simulators of the crew module, perfected spacewalking procedures underwater, and studied the Gaganyaan orbiter systems in detail. By early 2024, he had finished all rounds of training and was poised as one of the front-runners for

India's inaugural spaceflight. On 27 February 2024, Prime Minister Narendra Modi officially introduced Shubhanshu Shukla as one of the four astronauts designated for the Gaganyaan mission, publicly recognizing his role in India's human spaceflight team.

Even before Gaganyaan's own launch (planned for early 2027), Shukla's astronautical journey took a historic detour. ISRO decided to send one of its trained gaganyatris on a short-duration mission to the International Space Station in collaboration with the U.S. and commercial space company Axiom Space. Shukla was an obvious choice for this mission given his excellent performance and pilot background. Thus, in mid-2025, Group Captain Shubhanshu Shukla became the mission pilot of Axiom Mission 4 (Ax-4)—a privately organized flight that would carry a crew to the ISS for two weeks. When the SpaceX Falcon 9 rocket lifted off on 25 June 2025 from Kennedy Space Center with Shukla aboard the Crew Dragon capsule, India watched in collective awe and pride. For the first time in 41 years, an Indian citizen was heading into space.

Shukla's journey from Lucknow had literally reached orbit. Upon arrival at the ISS on 26 June 2025, he was welcomed and presented an astronaut pin as the 634th person to enter space. He conducted around 60 scientific experiments during his 18-day stay, including at least seven on behalf of ISRO in areas like life sciences and space agriculture. In accomplishing this mission, Shukla cemented his place in history as the first Indian astronaut to set foot on the ISS and the second Indian to travel to space (after Wing Commander Rakesh Sharma).

When Shukla addressed the nation from orbit, his words reflected the enormity of the moment and the humble beginnings that led there. 'Namaskar, my dear countrymen! What a ride... We are revolving around the Earth at 7.5 kilometres per second,' he exclaimed, the tricolour flag on his shoulder visible as he floated in microgravity. He emphasized that his journey was not just personal but belonged to all Indians—'This journey of mine is not a beginning to the International Space Station but to India's Human Space Programme. I want all of you to be part of this journey[...] Together, let's initiate India's Human Space Programme. Jai Hind!' In those words, one can sense the culmination of all the formative experiences that shaped him—the patriotic fervor sparked in 1999, the discipline forged at NDA, the daring of a fighter pilot and the curiosity of a lifelong student.

Foundation of a Space Farer

Shubhanshu Shukla's early life story is one of ambition met with action. From the playrooms and classrooms of Lucknow to the training fields of NDA and the cockpits of supersonic jets, each chapter added a layer of preparation for his ultimate role as an astronaut. His upbringing in a supportive, education-focused family gave him humility and focus. His schooling at CMS and the influences of war and airshows lit the fire of exploration in him. The audacity to secretly take the NDA exam at 16 showed his courage to chart his own path. Years of military training, combat flying, and advanced study then honed Shukla's skills and discipline to the highest degree. By the time the opportunity for spaceflight arrived, Shubhanshu stood ready to seize it—wearing, as one article aptly put it, 'his résumé on his uniform through the many badges of merit he'd earned.'

Shukla's journey illustrates how the formative experiences of youth can pave the way for extraordinary achievements. The same boy who once gazed at fighter planes in wonder ended up piloting spacecraft beyond Earth's atmosphere. His story has now become an inspiration to millions, especially in India—showing that with dedication, education and fearless persistence, even the most far-fetched childhood dreams (like touching the stars) can come true. As India progresses in human spaceflight, Shubhanshu Shukla's early life and career will be remembered as a blueprint for the country's future astronauts—start grounded in strong values and knowledge, then relentlessly reach for the sky.

Through every challenge and triumph in Shukla's early life, one constant shines—a quiet boy's unwavering resolve to aim high, work hard, and never give up. It is this resolve—nurtured in the alleys of Lucknow and tested in the skies—that carried Group Captain Shubhanshu Shukla to the ISS, making history and heralding a new era for India's space programme. His early life is not just a prelude to personal glory, but a launch pad for a nation's dreams, proving that the journey from a classroom to the cosmos is possible with the right mix of vision, courage and preparation.

2

From Cadet to Combat Pilot

Joining the NDA—A Cadet's Dawn

Shubhanshu Shukla stepped off the train in Pune with nothing but a small suitcase and a head full of dreams. It was a humid monsoon morning when he arrived at Khadakwasla, the home of India's prestigious National Defence Academy. As a 17-year-old fresh from Lucknow, he could hardly believe he had made it this far—and indeed, he nearly hadn't. Only months earlier, Shukla had secretly applied to NDA using a friend's form and sat for the entrance exam without telling his parents. His motivation ran deep—the televised bravery of soldiers during the 1999 Kargil War had lit a fire within him, as did an Air Force flying display he once watched wide-eyed as a schoolboy. Against odds, he passed the exam and secured admission. When his acceptance letter arrived, his family was stunned by the revelation—none more so than his father, Shambhu Dayal, a government clerk, and his mother Asha. Yet after the shock subsided, pride swelled. His elder sister Shuchi, who had quietly encouraged his ambitions all along, helped bridge the rift. In that moment, the trajectory of Shukla's life veered toward duty, discipline and a destiny he had only dared whisper to himself.

On his first day at NDA, Shukla felt both awe and apprehension. The NDA's campus sprawled 7,000 acres by the shimmering Khadakwasla Lake, dominated by the domed Sudan Block and manicured drill squares. The serenity of the Sahyadri Hills around them belied the intense regimen about to begin. Within hours of arrival, Shukla's civilian clothes were traded for an olive-green cadet uniform, his hair shorn to regulation length. Along with a throng of other nervous teenagers from every corner of India, he stood in formation as a booming voice called the first muster. In that sea of new faces, he realized they all shared a common resolve—to transform from boys into officers. The initial weeks hit him like a storm. Dawn started with a 4.30 a.m. trumpet reveille; by 5.00 a.m. he was out on the drill ground under a purple-gray sky, being barked at by drill instructors. The mornings smelled of wet grass and brasso polish, and echoed with shouted orders and the synchronized *thump* of boots on pavement. For Shukla, who had been a quiet, studious boy, this sudden immersion in military discipline was equally thrilling and daunting. Discipline became the new norm—beds had to be made with hospital corners tight enough to bounce a coin, shirts ironed razor-sharp, shoes gleaming like mirrors. Any infraction meant immediate push-ups or extra duties. He quickly learned to bear exhaustion with a grin. In rare private moments before collapsing into bed, he'd rub the blisters on his feet and remind himself why he came—to serve the nation that he had seen defended so bravely in Kargil, and to someday earn his wings as an Air Force pilot. Those thoughts sustained him through the toughest days.

Brotherhood in Hardship—Life as a Cadet

The life of an NDA cadet was a great equalizer. On the parade ground and in the barracks, it didn't matter where you came from—whether a farmer's son or a city student—everyone was pushed to their limits. Shukla found camaraderie in this shared struggle. In his squadron (appropriately named Hunter Squadron for the IAF cadets), he bonded with roommates over late-night study sessions and mutual grumbling about punishments. Together they endured punishing physical training—route marches that went on for 20 km under the blistering sun, obstacle courses that left them caked in mud, and endless rounds of push-ups and front-rolls ordered by senior cadets as 'extra instruction'. He vividly recalled one monsoon afternoon when he and his coursemates were ordered to lift their bicycles overhead and run laps in pouring rain—a traditional

NDA corrective measure known as 'cycle drill'. Arms trembling, several nearly gave up. Shukla too felt his strength failing, until a buddy beside him yelled over the rain, *'Lucknow, don't you dare stop!'* The nickname 'Lucknow' had stuck to Shukla, and hearing it in that moment sparked something. Gritting his teeth, he pushed on, one step at a time, matching pace with his friend. By the end of it, they were soaked, shivering, and utterly exhausted—but they had made it together. Through such trials, strangers became brothers. The cadets learned to laugh off hardship—aching muscles from morning PT, muddy uniforms from leopard-crawling through obstacle pits, even the occasional dressing-down by instructors—all became bonds of pride and memories to cherish.

Amid this rigorous lifestyle, Shukla went through a profound inner transformation. The shy boy from Lucknow steadily grew into a confident young man who could command a drill squad or lead a team in a mock combat exercise. In classes, he pursued his academics with the same quiet determination. NDA offered a Bachelor of Science degree through Jawaharlal Nehru University, and Shukla majored in Computer Science, often burning the midnight oil to balance studies with military training. The academy stressed that an officer must be as sharp of mind as of body. Shukla took that to heart, earning above-average grades. But it was outside the classroom, on the training fields, that he truly found his calling. He discovered a talent for navigation exercises and field tactics, displaying an analytical mind under pressure that impressed his instructors. More viscerally, he discovered a love for the skies.

Flight training at NDA was limited but pivotal. In the second year, as an Air Force cadet, Shukla got his first taste of actual flying in the academy's Super Dimona motor gliders. On a crisp morning, he took off in a tiny two-seater aircraft with an instructor by his side. As the ground fell away beneath him for the first time, Shukla's heart soared. High above the green hills, with the sun splitting through monsoon clouds, he felt an almost spiritual exhilaration—this is where he was meant to be. His instructor, Group Captain (Retd.) Anupam Banerjee, quickly noticed something special. 'He had a natural flair for flying... confident, intuitive—a very natural flier,' Banerjee would later recall of those early glider sorties. Indeed, while many cadets fumbled with the controls or felt airsick on their first flights, Shukla handled the craft smoothly, almost playfully banking and climbing as if he'd been born in a cockpit. He aced those initial flights, leaving Banerjee both astonished and pleased. What struck the veteran instructor even more was Shukla's attitude—sincere, hardworking and eager to learn, without a trace of arrogance about his abilities. After one particularly good flight, Banerjee told him during debrief, 'You'll go far if you keep this up. But remember, it's not enough to be a good flier or officer—you must be a good human being.' Those words etched themselves into Shukla's mind. Years later, as an astronaut-in-training, he sent a message thanking his old mentor for that lesson, a testament to how formative his NDA days truly were.

By the time Passing Out Parade arrived in spring 2005, Cadet Shukla had been thoroughly forged by the academy's tri-services crucible. On the parade ground in immaculate dress uniform, he and his batchmates marched past dignitaries and proud families with precision honed through blood, sweat and countless hours on the drill square. The thunder of 'Eyes... RIGHT!' and the crash of a thousand boots resonated in his very core. As the band played the NDA song one last time, Shukla's chest swelled with emotion. He stole a quick glance at the spectators' stands where he spotted his parents and siblings. His father—who once had misgivings about this path—stood beaming, eyes moist with pride. His mother folded her hands in silent prayer of thanks. And his sister Shuchi waved exuberantly, tears on her cheeks. Shukla felt a lump in his throat. In that moment, he reflected on the unlikely journey—from a quiet Lucknow boy filling out a secret application, to a confident young man saluting the Tricolour on these historic grounds. Discipline, camaraderie, service—these values were now ingrained in his soul. With a final toss of their caps into the air, the cadets became officers-in-the-making. Shukla graduated NDA with a BSc in Computer Science and, more importantly, the character needed to shoulder a national duty. Next stop—the Indian Air Force Academy, where his boyhood dream of flying fighter jets awaited realization.

Earning His Wings—Air Force Academy

In July 2005, Shukla arrived at the Indian Air Force Academy (AFA) in Dundigal, Telangana, for a year of specialized pilot training. If NDA had given him the backbone of an officer, AFA would give him the wings of a fighter pilot. The atmosphere at Dundigal was electric; cadets who had survived NDA's bootcamp were now about to live out their passion for flying. Shukla joined scores of fellow Air Force cadets—all sporting freshly stitched name badges and a mix of nervous and excited smiles—under the eagles emblem of the Academy. The training here was intense in a new way—days were packed with academics in aerodynamics, avionics, and aviation medicine, and mornings began on the tarmac instead of the parade ground. Shukla vividly remembers the first time he stood on the airfield at dawn, gazing at a line of trainer aircraft silhouetted against a pink sky, their aluminum skins glinting. The smell of aviation fuel, the whirr of ground crew prepping planes, and the distant roar of another cadet's engine starting up—these sensations sent a thrill through him. This was the world he had dreamed of.

Flying did not come easy, even for a 'natural' flier like Shukla. At the academy, he commenced basic flying training on a piston-engine propeller trainer (the venerable HPT-32 Deepak at that time, soon to be replaced by newer trainers). Day by day, sortie by sortie, he learned to take off, land and manoeuvre with precision. There were moments of frustration—a botched landing approach here, a navigation error there. Instructors were quick to bark criticisms over the radio or in post-flight debriefs, sparing no one's ego. Shukla swallowed each critique and returned the next day determined to improve. His experience with NDA's tough love had prepared him well—instead of wilting, he treated each mistake as a lesson, each success as motivation to push harder. Slowly, muscle memory and instinct fused; handling the aircraft became second nature. He learned to trust his training and his machine, to keep cool when a stall warning blared or when buffeted by crosswinds on final approach.

Then came the red-letter day of every pilot's life—the first solo flight. After months of dual instruction, Shukla's flight instructor finally stepped out and patted the aircraft's side, signaling Shukla to take her up alone. Heart pounding with a mix of fear and exhilaration, Shukla completed his pre-flight checks meticulously (perhaps double and triple-checking in his nervousness). He taxied to the runway, requested clearance, and pushed the throttle forward. As the little trainer lifted off the ground carrying only him, Shukla felt a liberating rush—a burst of pure confidence that *Yes, I can do this on my own*. Up in the blue sky, alone in the cockpit for the first time, he noticed how peaceful it was at altitude. The clutter of instructions and constant evaluation was momentarily absent; it was just him and the aeroplane. He conducted the required circuit pattern, and the radio crackled with the Air Traffic Control officer wishing him luck. On final approach, the runway loomed—he focused intensely—throttling back, aligning perfectly, controlling descent rate… *thump!* The wheels kissed the tarmac in a smooth touchdown. A wave of triumph washed over him. Taxiing back, he was greeted by the ritual most pilots cherish— fellow cadets and instructors dousing him with buckets of cold water and hearty slaps on the back—the traditional celebration for a successful first solo. Shukla's grin was ear to ear as he stood soaked on the ramp, knowing this was a rite of passage he'd remember forever.

After basic training came advanced jet training. The Indian Air Force introduced the British-made Hawk advanced jet trainer around those years, but Shukla's cohort also trained on the indigenous Kiran MkII jets for weapons and tactics. Transitioning from a slow propeller plane to a fast jet was like going from a bicycle to a race car. The speed and complexity jumped dramatically. Suddenly he was dealing with jet thrust, G-forces pinning him to his seat during combat manoeuvres, and a dizzying array of dials and sensors. Shukla loved every second of it. He learned to execute aerobatic manoeuvres—loops, barrel rolls, the split-S—painting white contrails in the sky over Dundigal's training airspace. Yet the training was unforgiving. On one high-G turn during air combat manoeuvring practice, Shukla blacked out for a couple of seconds—a sobering lesson in the importance of physical conditioning and the anti-G straining manoeuvres pilots must perform to keep blood flowing to the brain. He hit the gym with renewed vigor after that, determined that G-forces would never get the better of him again.

All through, camaraderie kept flourishing. In the evenings, the cadets would gather, still buzzing from the day's flights, to compare notes and occasional bruises. They helped each other study aircraft systems late into the night or practise emergency procedures ('engine flame-out at takeoff, what do you do?') with one acting as instructor and the other as hapless student. In these exchanges, Shukla often emerged as a calm leader, helping clarify concepts for others. His mates noticed he was uncommonly composed even after turbulent flights, always the one to crack a light joke to ease everyone's nerves. Still, he wasn't above youthful mischief—there was the time he and a friend 'borrowed' an extra dessert from the mess to fuel a late-night study session, only to end up doing extra drills as penance when caught. Small adventures like that kept them human amidst the military rigours.

At last, in June 2006, Shukla reached the culmination of this phase—commissioning as an officer in the Indian

Air Force. The Air Force Academy's Commissioning Parade was a spectacle of aerial flypasts and immaculate marching. Dressed in air force blue with his shiny new officer's insignia on the shoulders, Shukla took the oath to serve the Constitution of India and protect its sovereignty—a solemn vow resonating with the theme of national duty he had long embraced. As he strode up to receive his *wings*—the pilot's brevet badge—his family pinned it on his chest in a proud emotional moment. He was now officially Flying Officer Shubhanshu Shukla, posted to the fighter stream of the IAF. The child who once folded paper planes on Lucknow rooftops was now a fighter pilot for India.

Skies of Steel—Fighter Pilot in the Making

Shukla's early years in the IAF took him across the length and breadth of India as he trained and served on various fighter aircraft. After commissioning, he underwent Operational Conversion—essentially learning to apply his training to real combat aircraft. His first assignment was with a frontline squadron flying the MiG-21 'Bison', a supersonic interceptor famed for its unforgiving nature. The MiG-21 was a tiny, lightning-fast jet—often likened to a high-powered rocket with razor-sharp wings. Many young pilots found it daunting, but Shukla approached it with a mix of respect and eagerness. Under the tutelage of seasoned squadron instructors, he learned the quirks of this legendary aircraft. He experienced the raw thrill of breaking the sound barrier for the first time in a MiG-21—one moment pressing through thick air, the next moment a thunderous boom trailing behind as the aircraft crossed Mach 1, pushing into a realm he had only imagined. It was exhilarating, yet he understood why the MiG-21 demanded absolute precision; a mistake at those speeds could be deadly. Shukla's discipline served him well—he listened carefully in briefing rooms, memorized emergency checklists by heart and practised simulation after simulation. Before long, he was performing solo interceptions and gunnery exercises, honing the hunter's edge every fighter pilot needs.

Over the next few years, Shukla expanded his repertoire. The IAF rotated him through multiple aircraft to broaden his experience—a testament to his skill and adaptability. He trained on the twin-engine MiG-29 Fulcrum, experiencing its blistering thrust and excellent dogfighting agility. He spent time on the SEPECAT Jaguar, a deep-strike bomber, learning the art of low-level penetration and precision strike flying. He also flew the BAE Hawk advanced jet (likely as an instructor or in training roles) which, compared to the fighters, felt almost docile but was excellent for refining technique. Each platform taught him something new—the MiG-29 taught him high-altitude dogfights, the Jaguar taught navigation at tree-top heights, and the Hawk reinforced fundamentals. By the time he became a fully operational fighter pilot, Shukla had accumulated hundreds of hours in fighter cockpits, building towards the 2,000 flight hours he would later log in his career.

Shukla's home units became his new family. In those early years as a young officer in a fighter squadron, he learned the value of teamwork and trust in an entirely new dimension. Flying in a two-ship or four-ship formation, he and his wingmen depended on each other with their lives. They would brief together, fly together and debrief every detail. Shukla particularly remembered an intense training exercise over the deserts of Rajasthan. His section was simulating a combat air patrol when they were 'bounced' by a pair of instructor aircraft playing enemy. In the mock dogfight that ensued, Shukla had a MiG-21 on his tail. Heart pounding, he instinctively broke hard into the attacker—the g-forces squeezing him as he jinked and pulled. His wingman, following doctrine, swooped in to chase the bogey off Shukla's tail, freeing Shukla to reverse and *'gun'* the now-distracted opponent. The exercise ended in their favor. In the debrief, the flight lead commended their teamwork—neither had tried to be a lone hero; instead they had supported each other flawlessly. It was a proud moment that cemented Shukla's belief in camaraderie and trust as the core of military aviation. He also learned humility—on another occasion, a senior pilot outfoxed him easily in a dogfight exercise, teaching Shukla that there is always more to learn and that split-second decisions can make the difference.

Each experience, good or bad, was adding to his inner transformation—tempering his confidence with wisdom.

Beyond training, the life of a fighter pilot also involved national duty in very tangible ways. Shukla participated in numerous readiness drills and border patrol missions during tense periods. He was still a junior pilot around the time when, in the late 2000s and 2010s, the security situation occasionally spiked. Once, during an escalation of cross-border tensions, Shukla's squadron was scrambled on high alert. Sitting strapped in his cockpit at dusk, engine whining ready for immediate takeoff, he felt the weight of responsibility like never before. Though the crisis de-escalated before any engagement, those long hours on standby, watching the sun dip below the horizon while his fighter jet idled on the runway, left a deep impression. He realized that everything he had trained for—every push-up, every late-night study, every simulated sortie—was ultimately to be ready when the nation called. The Tricolour painted on his aircraft's tail was not just decoration; it was a trust. He vowed, as many pilots silently do, that if the time came, he would perform his duty with honour and without hesitation.

His professional excellence did not go unnoticed. Superiors noted Shukla's blend of skill, composure and leadership potential. As he rose to the rank of Flight Lieutenant and then Squadron Leader, he often found himself mentoring newer pilots, much as his seniors had mentored him. He had a patient teaching style and could convey tactics clearly. On the ground, he was popular in the crew room—quick to help plan missions, meticulous in his paperwork, and known to play a mean game of squash or volleyball in unit sports meets. Off duty, he remained the humble, grounded person he'd always been. Colleagues recall that Shukla rarely boasted about his exploits; if anything, he was more likely to credit his team or crack a joke at his own expense. This combination of quiet confidence and approachability made him well-liked and respected in equal measure.

Forging an Ace—TACDE and the Making of a Combat Leader

By his middle years of service, Shukla had proven himself to be among the IAF's best and brightest. This earned him a coveted opportunity to attend the Tactics and Combat Development Establishment (TACDE)—India's very own 'Top Gun' school for fighter pilots. TACDE (pronounced '*Tack-dee*') is where the top 1% of IAF aviators are sent to become fighter combat leaders, honing exceptional aerial tactics and instructor skills. Shukla knew that TACDE would be a whole new crucible, one that would test everything he had learned so far and then some. In 2014, he reported to the airbase in Gwalior where TACDE is headquartered. Gwalior's baking summer heat and infamous crosswinds would be his new training companions. The base buzzed with activity—here, experienced pilots from various squadrons converged to pit their skills against each other and to learn advanced combat science. Shukla felt a mix of excitement and humility—he was surrounded by aces and decorated instructors, and now he had to prove he belonged among them.

The TACDE syllabus was intense both in air and on ground. By day, Shukla flew high-octane sorties, often in aircraft like the Sukhoi Su-30MKI—the IAF's premier air superiority fighter known for its thrust-vectoring agility. By night, he pored over tactics manuals and engagement debriefs, sometimes until the early hours. Every mission in TACDE was a simulated war scenario. One afternoon, Shukla found himself in a 1-versus-2 dogfight exercise, taking on two 'aggressor' jets with just his single Su-30. It was a test of situational awareness and nerve. As the mock enemy jets locked onto him, Shukla remembered a legendary manoeuvre taught at TACDE—the 'Cobra' manoeuvre, wherein a Su-30 pilot can suddenly raise the jet's nose to an extreme angle, bleeding off speed and causing a pursuer to overshoot. With a deep breath and steady hands, he executed it. For a heartbeat, his aircraft seemingly defied aerodynamics—nose pointed skyward, screeching at the edge of a stall—and the chasing jet shot past harmlessly. Shukla then rolled behind that jet, 'destroying' it in the exercise, before swiftly evading the second. The debrief was full of adrenaline and analysis, and Shukla earned a nod from the chief instructor for pulling off an expert-level tactic. But TACDE was as much about learning humility as showcasing skill. In other sorties, he occasionally found himself 'shot down' in simulations by cunning peers who exploited any mistake. Each loss taught him new ways to refine his reaction time and tactical thinking.

On the ground, TACDE fostered an almost academic environment—except the academics were life-and-death air combat lessons. Shukla dove into studying radar theory, missile envelopes and even enemy air force tactics from around the world. In joint sessions, he debated strategies with fellow trainees, sometimes passionately arguing the fine points of beyond-visual-range engagement or low-level evasion. In this collegial yet competitive arena, he further sharpened his leadership qualities. Mid-way through the course, teams were assigned a project—to devise and present a new combat training module for their squadrons. Shukla was chosen to lead one such team. He guided his teammates in pooling their collective experience—one had expertise in electronic warfare, another in mountain flying—and together they crafted a comprehensive module on 'Night-time Multi-Bogey Engagement Tactics.' Shukla presented it to a panel of senior officers, confidently and clearly. It was well-received and even slated for implementation in a few squadrons. This was a proud moment; not only had he proven his mettle in the cockpit, but he had also contributed to the Air Force's tactical evolution.

Graduating from TACDE, Shukla earned the formal title of Fighter Combat Leader, marking him as an elite tactician and instructor. He returned to the IAF not just as an ace pilot, but as a force multiplier—someone expected to elevate others. True enough, he soon took on roles as a flight commander and instructor in his squadron. Younger pilots sought him out for advice on combat manoeuvres, and Shukla was generous in imparting the knowledge gleaned from TACDE. His reports note that he could dissect a complex dogfight situation on the debrief board with clarity, turning it into a lesson for all. Through TACDE, the theme of camaraderie took on a higher form for Shukla—it was now about imparting lessons and lifting up the entire team, not just camaraderie in shared hardship but camaraderie in pursuit of excellence.

Testing the Limits—A Test Pilot's Journey

Having mastered combat flying and tactics, Shukla's hunger for growth led him to yet another elite avenue—the world of flight testing. He was selected to attend the Aircraft and Systems Testing Establishment (ASTE) to train as a test pilot, one of the most demanding and prestigious roles for an aviator. If TACDE was about squeezing maximum performance out of known aircraft, ASTE was about diving into the unknown—flying new or modified aircraft, pushing them to and beyond limits to ensure they were safe and effective for the rest of the force. Becoming a test pilot would require Shukla to channel not just his flying prowess but also his scientific acumen and engineering insight. Always a keen student, Shukla embraced the challenge fully. He pursued a master's degree during this period to bolster his technical foundation. The balancing of coursework and flight duties was tough, but by now Shukla had the stamina and discipline of a seasoned warrior-scholar.

At ASTE in Bengaluru, Shukla encountered a different pace of Air Force life. The work was meticulous and often less publicly glamorous, but no less thrilling for those involved. He joined small teams working on cutting-edge projects—integrating a new radar on a fighter jet, testing a more powerful engine variant, or fine-tuning the flight control software of a new indigenous aircraft. Each day's flying came with a detailed test card—specific manoeuvres to perform, data points to collect, often at the edges of the flight envelope. Shukla might be found one day climbing to 50,000 feet in a modified MiG to test its engine performance in thin air, and the next day skimming the tree-tops in a Dornier turboprop to assess stability with a new payload configuration. The variety was immense. He even got to fly foreign aircraft on exchange trials, broadening his experience further. In one notable trial, Shukla helped test an advanced pilot ejection seat system. This involved a series of high-risk exercises—steep climbs and intentionally induced spins to see if the ejection system would function under extreme attitudes. It was hair-raising work—he once went into an unrecoverable spin deliberately, trusting the theories and procedures, and only punched out of it at the last safe moment. But the data he collected helped engineers refine the safety systems that would protect future pilots.

Colleagues at ASTE noted Shukla's calm bravery and analytical mind. After each flight, he would sit with engineers to debrief, translating the visceral feel of the aircraft into technical feedback—did a new control surface flutter? Was there unexpected vibration at high speed? He had a knack for communicating these observations in precise detail, a crucial skill for a test pilot. It saved time and guided design corrections accurately. Over time, Shukla became one of ASTE's go-to officers for critical test missions. He flew everything from the workhorse An-32 transport (assessing avionics upgrades) to the latest variant of the Sukhoi Su-30MKI (perhaps in weapons trials). This breadth made him a repository of flying knowledge.

Yet amidst test runs and engineer meetings, Shukla never lost sight of the larger purpose. In the quiet moments after a successful test flight, he'd step out onto the dispersal and look at the hangar where a prototype sat glinting. He felt a swell of pride knowing that his work was helping the nation become self-reliant in defense technology—whether by proving an indigenous system or validating a crucial modification. National duty took a new form here—not aerial dogfights but painstaking innovation and safety for others. This, too, was service to the nation, and Shukla gave it his all.

The test pilot years also brought personal growth in other ways. Bengaluru, being a science and technology hub, connected Shukla with many bright minds. He found himself collaborating with civilian scientists and even participating in seminars. Always modest, he occasionally marveled that this once upon-a-time quiet boy from Lucknow was now co-authoring a technical paper on flight stability, or giving a talk on cockpit human-factors to a room of engineers. It was also during these years that Shukla married Dr Kamna, a dentist, and started a family—a grounding force in his life. Balancing high-octane flying and home life was challenging, but Kamna's unwavering support became his anchor. On days when a risky test flight loomed, a quick morning call with his wife or a playful exchange with his young son reminded him of what he was working to protect. These gentle flashbacks to his Lucknow upbringing and family values—such as his mother's voice reminding him to stay humble, or his father's emphasis on doing any job thoroughly—provided emotional sustenance even as he ventured into ever more demanding roles.

By 2019, Group Captain Shubhanshu Shukla (he had risen in rank over the years, reaching Wing Commander and then Group Captain by March 2024) was a richly seasoned officer. He was a test pilot with over 2,000 flight hours on more than half a dozen aircraft types, a fighter combat leader respected for his tactical brilliance, and a mentor figure to many. These years of discipline, camaraderie, transformation and service had molded him into an exceptional candidate for an extraordinary mission that lay ahead.

Foundations for the Final Frontier

Shukla often reflected on the seemingly disparate threads of his career—the harsh discipline of NDA, the camaraderie of squadron life, the strategic mindset from TACDE, the technical mastery as a test pilot—and realized they all converged into a singular tapestry of growth. Unbeknownst to him, this tapestry was exactly what India's space agency, ISRO, was seeking as it quietly scouted for talent to crew the nation's first human spaceflight programme. In 2019, the call of destiny came. The Institute of Aerospace Medicine (IAM) in Bengaluru, in cooperation with the Indian Air Force, shortlisted a handful of elite pilots for India's ambitious Gaganyaan project—the quest to send Indians into space on an indigenous spacecraft. Group Captain Shukla's name was right at the top of that list. When Shukla received the official communication, he was momentarily stunned. He had always looked up to Wing Commander Rakesh Sharma, who in 1984 became the first Indian in space. But Sharma's voyage was a once-in-a-generation event under a foreign programme. Now, over four decades later, India was launching its own astronauts. The little boy who had gazed at stars from his Lucknow rooftop and dreamed while watching Kargil heroes on TV realized that fate had been quietly grooming him for this honour all along.

He went home that evening and shared the news with his wife and family. There were tears, hugs, and laughter—a mix of excitement and the weight of knowing challenges ahead. His parents, hearing that their son might go to space, were at first anxious but ultimately filled with pride; they recalled how they had once been apprehensive about him even joining the military, and now he was on the verge of making history. Shuchi, his sister, couldn't help but tease, 'So the secret NDA application was just the beginning of your surprises, huh?' They all knew Shukla would approach this next journey with the same quiet grit he had shown since that day he mailed off an application form as a teen.

In the following months, Shukla joined three other selected IAF officers for basic astronaut training—an odyssey that would take him from the centrifuges and simulators of Russia's Yuri Gagarin Cosmonaut Training Center to the labs of ISRO in India. But that story would be another chapter. As he prepared to leave for Russia, Shukla took one last solitary walk on the airfield at the test squadron in Bengaluru. Dusk was falling, and a lone fighter jet in the distance roared into the sky. He paused, watching the silhouette dart among the evening clouds, and thought of all the phases of life that had led him here. Discipline, camaraderie, inner transformation, national duty—these had been his guiding stars. They had steeled his body, nourished his soul, and ignited his sense of purpose. They had turned a shy Lucknow boy into an Air Force Group Captain trusted to don the nation's flag in outer space.

He closed his eyes and saw flashes of memory—the NDA parade ground and a younger him standing at attention; the cramped cockpit of a MiG-21 and the elation of that first sonic boom; the faces of friends who flew wingtip to wingtip with him through danger; the stern yet caring voice of his TACDE instructor discussing a manoeuvre late into the night; the concentrated gaze of an engineer as he reported a test result; and beyond them all, the faces of his family, beaming with encouragement. All these moments were his strength. As Shukla opened his eyes, he felt ready. A gentle night breeze swept across the tarmac, almost as if whispering a benediction. In that breeze, one could imagine the voices of his past—instructors, comrades, loved ones—urging him onward. The stars were emerging overhead. Shubhanshu Shukla straightened his back, a quiet smile on his face, and murmured the phrase that had become a personal mantra: *Service before self.* With that, India's decorated fighter pilot turned astronaut-candidate stepped forward into the twilight, poised to embrace the challenges of the final frontier, armed with the lessons forged from NDA to the skies and a spirit transformed for the greater glory of the nation.

3

Becoming Gaganyatri: The Astronaut Transformation

When the Indian Space Research Organisation (ISRO) officially announced Group Captain Shubhanshu Shukla as one of four astronauts for its inaugural Gaganyaan crew in February 2024, it marked a historic turning point. In a ceremony at the Vikram Sarabhai Space Centre in Thiruvananthapuram, Prime Minister Narendra Modi introduced the nation's first set of 'gaganyatris'—literally *sky-travelers*—and awarded them astronaut wings. For Shubhanshu, an Indian Air Force test pilot, this was more than a new assignment. It was the culmination of years of grueling preparation and personal transformation. He was no longer training merely to fly aircraft; he was preparing to leave Earth's atmosphere entirely. This chapter explores Shubhanshu's journey through intensive training in Russia and India, the media frenzy that greeted him after the announcement, and his internal evolution from a fighter pilot to an astronaut on the cusp of launch.

From Top Gun to Astronaut Candidate

Long before he was selected for spaceflight, Shubhanshu Shukla had proven himself among India's best aviators. Inspired as a teenager by the bravery of Indian soldiers in the 1999 Kargil War, Shubhanshu set his sights on a life of service and adventure. A famous family story illustrates his single-minded determination—on the morning of his elder sister's *vidaai* (wedding send-off) in 2001, 16-year-old Shubhanshu slipped away from home without telling anyone. As relatives grew concerned at his absence, he was furiously pedaling his bicycle across Lucknow to take the entrance exam for the National Defence Academy (NDA). 'He left the wedding to give the exam,' his sister recounted later, describing how he secretly obtained the application form with a friend's help. Shubhanshu returned home only after finishing the test, nonchalantly telling his shocked family, 'I am here, now tell me what to do'. In that moment, it became clear that when Shubhanshu set a goal, nothing—not even a family celebration—would deter him from pursuing it.

Shubhanshu aced the NDA exam and was accepted into India's elite military academy, graduating in 2004 with a bachelor's degree in computer science. He earned his commission as an Indian Air Force fighter pilot in 2006. Over the next decade, Shubhanshu built an impressive resume, flying over 2,000 hours on a variety of aircraft—from nimble MiG-21 and MiG-29 fighters to heavy An-32 transports. He became a Test Pilot and an instructor at the IAF's prestigious Tactics and Combat Development Establishment (TACDE), India's 'Top Gun' school. At TACDE, only the top 1% of pilots hone advanced aerial combat tactics, and Shubhanshu emerged as one of those elite flyers. This wealth of experience would later prove vital; extensive flying hours and superb technical skills were baseline requirements for the astronauts of Gaganyaan. Still, being a stellar pilot was just the starting point. To become an astronaut, Shubhanshu would have to push himself far beyond the cockpit, into realms of science, survival and space systems engineering that few military men ever tread.

In 2018, as ISRO ramped up its human spaceflight programme, Shubhanshu quietly put himself forward for the astronaut selection process. True to his habit of 'silent determination,' he didn't even tell his family at first—much as he hadn't told them about the NDA exam years earlier. Screening was rigorous. ISRO's Institute of Aerospace Medicine (IAM) evaluated hundreds of candidates on criteria ranging from flight experience to physical fitness and psychological resilience. Shubhanshu, with nearly 15 years of distinguished service and a flawless health record, quickly made the shortlists. By late 2019, he was among the final 12 candidates, and soon one of the final four chosen to form India's first astronaut cadre. At age 34, he was younger than the officially recommended age (ISRO had indicated astronaut applicants should be around 39), but his qualifications were undeniable. The 'Gaganyaan Group 1'—as the four would be known—comprised Shubhanshu and three fellow pilots (Prashanth Nair, Angad Pratap, and Ajit Krishnan), all with extensive flying backgrounds. In early 2020, these four men stood on the brink of a bold new chapter. They were about to trade their fighter jets for spacecraft simulators, and their comfortable lives in India for a year in Star City, Russia, the cradle of cosmonaut training.

Star City: Baptism by Spacefaring Fire

Shubhanshu's astronaut transformation began in earnest in January 2020, when he and the other three Gaganyaan candidates departed for Zvyozdny Gorodok, better known as Star City, near Moscow. This storied site had trained every Russian cosmonaut since Yuri Gagarin, as well as international astronauts (including India's own Rakesh Sharma in the 1980s). Now it would train Shubhanshu Shukla and his teammates, who arrived with a mix of excitement and resolve. They knew the coming months would test every aspect of their being. Basic training in Russia was slated to last about 11-12 months—an intensive course covering astronautical theory, physical conditioning, and survival skills for spaceflight.

The training kicked off on 10 February 2020. Almost immediately, the candidates were thrust into extreme environments designed to simulate the stresses of space.

One of the first ordeals was high-G centrifuge training, spinning them in giant centrifuges to reproduce the crushing forces of rocket launch and re-entry. As the G-forces mounted, Shubhanshu had to resist the blood draining from his head and stay conscious, practising the straining manoeuvres he'd learned as a fighter pilot. But even his Top Gun days hadn't put his body through sustained G-loads like this. Such drills were essential to condition the astronauts' cardiovascular systems and prevent blackouts during the real launch. Shubhanshu later reflected that they 'train for all kinds of emergency situations,' and indeed the Russian curriculum left nothing to chance. Besides centrifuge rides, it included exposure to weightlessness and violent motion to provoke disorientation—all to prepare them for space's challenges.

One unforgettable experience was the parabolic flight campaign. Strapped inside a special Ilyushin-76 aircraft, Shubhanshu and his colleagues flew repeated parabolic arcs that briefly switched gravity off, turning the cabin into a playground of floating objects and tumbling bodies. These zero-G periods lasted only 20-30 seconds at a time, but they gave the trainees their first taste of true weightlessness. Shubhanshu found it exhilarating but also disorienting. In microgravity, even simple tasks like orienting one's body or capturing a floating pen demanded new techniques. By the end of those flights, though, the Indians could somersault and manoeuvre with growing confidence. This was more than just fun—it was crucial practice in adapting to a sensation that would be constant once they reached orbit.

Survival training formed another core pillar of the Russian programme. The 'what if' scenarios of spaceflight can be daunting—a capsule might land off-course in a remote wilderness or splash down far from recovery teams. To build survival skills and teamwork under duress, the instructors sent Shubhanshu and the others into harsh terrains with minimal supplies. In one winter exercise, they were left in a dense forest during sub-zero temperatures, mimicking a capsule landing in the Siberian taiga. Bundled in insulating suits and surrounded by snow and silence, they learned to erect a rudimentary shelter out of spacecraft parachute silk, gather firewood and ration their emergency provisions. Huddling around a small fire under the Russian night sky, Shubhanshu had time to reflect on the surreal path that had led him there—an Indian pilot learning to survive a frozen night, all in preparation for space. Another exercise dropped them into water with full flight suits on, to simulate an ocean splashdown. They practised clambering into life rafts and staying afloat until rescue, all while waves tossed them about. Such water survival tasks, combined with swimming tests in spacesuit mockups, ensured the crew could handle an emergency sea landing.

Adding to the physical tests were intense classroom sessions. Despite the language barrier, Shubhanshu diligently absorbed lessons in basic astronautics, orbital mechanics and spacecraft systems. The Russians introduced him to the layout and operation of a Soyuz spacecraft—not because he would fly one, but as a proxy to understand spacecraft anatomy and crew functions. Since future missions could involve working with international partners, the trainees also got exposure to each other's languages and procedures. (Typically, cosmonauts learn some English and astronauts learn some Russian; the Indians likely picked up a bit of Russian along the way.) Through it all, Shubhanshu's inherent discipline shone. In his off-hours, he kept up a strict fitness regimen in Star City's gymnasium—running, weightlifting, and endurance training to meet the lofty physical standards required. The strict physical training programme was non-negotiable; an astronaut's body must be robust enough to handle launch pressures and the muscle-atrophy of weightlessness.

Perhaps the most subtle challenges were psychological. To test and enhance their mental resilience, Shubhanshu and his comrades underwent isolation and stress tests. In one scenario, they were confined in a mock spacecraft module for days, with scripted emergencies thrown at them to gauge reactions. In another, they faced simulations of system failures and had to work calmly under ticking clocks. Psychological evaluations ensured they could maintain composure, make decisions and cooperate as a team under extreme pressure. Here, Shubhanshu's patient, thoughtful nature helped. Those who know him often describe him as 'quiet, deeply thoughtful and focused'—traits that were now being honed to razor-sharpness. Star City's instructors were impressed that the Indians never cracked—no one quit or fell apart, even when COVID-19 briefly interrupted training in 2020. The pandemic lockdowns forced a pause, but also perhaps gave the astronauts a taste of isolation and adaptability in a very real sense. As soon as restrictions eased, they were back in the simulators and classrooms, catching up rapidly on lost time.

After nearly a year of this demanding regimen, victory was at hand. By March 2021, Shubhanshu and the others had completed their basic training in Russia. Dmitry Rogozin, head of Roscosmos, personally congratulated the 'Indian gaganauts' on finishing the course, praising their health and fitness. It was a proud moment—the four men had proven themselves capable in every trial Star City had thrown at them. They were now certified astronaut trainees. Shubhanshu in particular had emerged as a natural leader within the group, often the steadying voice during tense simulations, thanks to his experience and calm demeanour. In their final weeks in Russia, the team even got to enjoy small perks—a photograph captures Shubhanshu at Gagarin's famed statue in Star City, smiling modestly in his blue training jumpsuit. The sense of camaraderie between the four was evident—they had become like brothers through this shared baptism by fire.

When Shubhanshu touched back down on Indian

soil in spring 2021, he was a changed man. He had left as an ace pilot; he returned as a fully trained astronaut-candidate, or *vyomanaut* in popular Indian parlance. Yet this was only base camp on the ascent to space. Ahead loomed the Everest of mission-specific training, now to be undertaken in India, tailored for the exact spacecraft and mission profile of Gaganyaan. Still, the hardest part—transforming these IAF officers into spacefarers—was well underway. As Shubhanshu's team prepared for the next phase, they carried with them the confidence built in Star City. They had held their own in the same halls where Gagarin and Sharma once trained. The dream of hoisting the Tiranga (tricolour flag) in space felt closer than ever.

Mission-Specific Training on Home Soil

Back home, ISRO wasted no time moving the gaganyatris into mission-specific preparation. The Gaganyaan crew capsule and its systems were indigenous and unique, so Shubhanshu needed to master an entirely new spacecraft—one still in development. For this, ISRO established its own Astronaut Training Facility in Bengaluru. Throughout 2021 and 2022, while engineers toiled to human-rate the Gaganyaan capsule and rocket, Shubhanshu and his colleagues dived into learning every nut and bolt of the mission.

In Bengaluru, they trained on crew module

simulators, studying the layout of controls and displays that they would use in orbit. They rehearsed normal flight sequences as well as every conceivable malfunction. Under the guidance of ISRO's Human Spaceflight Centre, Shubhanshu practised procedures like manual orbital corrections, life-support management, and emergency responses inside the capsule. As an aviator, he was used to cockpits, but the Gaganyaan capsule's confined space and system intricacies required a different mindset. He had to become as much an engineer as a pilot—able to troubleshoot environmental control systems or computer glitches on the fly. To bolster his technical acumen, Shubhanshu even enrolled in an advanced degree. Amid training, he pursued and completed a master's in Aerospace Engineering from the Indian Institute of Science. Balancing academics with practical drills was tough, but it paid off—he gained deeper understanding of spacecraft design, orbital dynamics, and materials—knowledge that would help him operate the capsule more effectively.

The training in India also emphasized team coordination for the mission. ISRO hadn't yet publicly decided whether all four astronauts would fly—in fact, it was expected that only three would be aboard the first crewed flight, with the fourth as a reserve. Regardless, the quartet trained together, rotating through various crew roles. Shubhanshu was often slotted as Mission Pilot, effectively second-in-command of the spacecraft.

His job would be to support the mission commander (possibly one of the group captains) in monitoring the spacecraft, and to take over manual control if needed. Countless simulation runs forged their crew resource management skills—clear communication, task-sharing and backing each other up under pressure. Having known each other for years now, a natural chemistry existed—a quiet nod or single code word in the simulator was enough for Shubhanshu to coordinate with Angad or Prashanth during a simulated anomaly. In debriefs, instructors commended how teamwork and support had become second nature to them. This bond would be a lifeline in space, where isolated crews depend only on each other.

Another critical aspect was training for space experiments and EVA (extra-vehicular activity) contingencies. Although the first Gaganyaan was a short orbital mission (planned for 3–7 days in low Earth orbit), ISRO intended the crew to perform a set of microgravity experiments during that time. Shubhanshu and his crewmates were briefed on experiments ranging from biological studies to material science payloads that would ride with them. They learned how to handle experiment kits in weightlessness, how to record observations, and how to stow samples securely. Each astronaut took lead on certain experiments; Shubhanshu, with his penchant for detail, was assigned a few that matched his background (possibly ones involving fluid dynamics or mechanical systems given his engineering focus). They practised these in a neutral buoyancy lab—a large water tank in Bengaluru—where partial gravity simulation helped them get a feel for performing tasks without full weight support. Though actual spacewalks were not planned for this mission, ISRO still gave basic spacewalk training with a dummy spacesuit underwater, to cover worst-case scenarios. If something forced an EVA or hatch operation in orbit, they would have the fundamental skills to execute it.

Even the mundane was rehearsed—eating and hygiene in space were new experiences that training covered. ISRO's food and nutrition labs worked with the crew on space-safe Indian meals (like paratha and curry sealed in retort pouches!). Shubhanshu sampled these during training and provided feedback—after all, staying well-nourished and healthy was part of an astronaut's job. He also underwent sessions on meditation and mental wellness, guided by psychologists to cope with confined living. This was still Earth, but they simulated orbital living by staying for 2–3 days inside a habitat module mock-up, running on mission timeline (with 90-minute 'orbit' cycles to mirror sunrise/sunset every 90 minutes in orbit). Shubhanshu took these exercises seriously, often volunteering for extra hours in the simulator to refine his response to alarms or to practise donning the orange pressure suit in under five minutes (a required speed in emergencies). Every drill, no matter how routine, brought him one step closer to being flight-ready.

By the end of 2023, Shubhanshu had spent nearly four years in continuous astronaut training—first abroad, then domestically. He had transformed physically—his fitness was at an all-time peak, muscles honed by daily workouts to counteract the muscle atrophy space can cause. Mentally, he was now fluent in the language of space operations and could likely recite spacecraft checklists in his sleep. This period also included personal growth of a different sort—Shubhanshu became adept at juggling multiple roles: student, engineer, public figure and family man (albeit from a distance). His wife and young son had seen little of him during training stints, a sacrifice he was keenly aware of. He kept in touch via video calls whenever possible, but the mission came first. 'He has been undergoing rigorous training for a year-and-a-half and has not met his family during this period,' a June 2025 report noted. The astronaut's path demanded such trade-offs, and Shubhanshu managed them with quiet fortitude.

The Spotlight: Unveiling the Gaganyatris

Throughout the training phase, ISRO had kept the identities of the astronaut candidates fairly low-profile. That changed dramatically on 27 February 2024, when Prime Minister Modi publicly *unveiled the names* of the four gaganyatris. Overnight, Shubhanshu Shukla became a household name across India. The event itself was televised live. In front of rows of scientists and officials, Shubhanshu and his three comrades stood in formal blue uniforms as the Prime Minister introduced each one to the nation. 'They are four forces that encompass the aspirations of 1.4 billion people,' Modi proclaimed, lauding the team. In that moment, Shubhanshu felt the weight of a nation's expectations settle on his shoulders. He was proud, certainly—proud to be representing India at the final frontier—but he also felt a jolt of reality. This was *real* now, no longer a quiet training programme in the shadows. The world knew his name and face.

The media reaction was immediate and intense. Within hours, news crews descended on Shubhanshu's hometown in Lucknow, hoping to interview anyone who knew him. Similar scenes played out in the hometowns of Nair, Pratap and Krishnan. For example, in Nair's village in Kerala, neighbours and friends gathered to celebrate, recalling his childhood and expressing pride. In Shubhanshu's case, his parents and sisters were suddenly thrust into the limelight back in Uttar Pradesh. While they were immensely proud—'He's carrying the hopes of a billion Indians,' his sister Shuchi would later say—the attention was overwhelming for a family that had largely kept his mission low-key. TV channels replayed file photos of Shubhanshu in his Air Force flying suit, headlines dubbed him 'India's next space hero', and social media erupted in congratulatory messages.

The celebrity status of the astronauts prompted even the Prime Minister to urge caution. Modi publicly requested that people allow the astronauts to train without disturbance, acknowledging that too much fanfare could distract them. 'I urge all people, including media professionals, to allow them to do their duties without hindrances. It's the beginning of the real story. Let's support them to the fullest,' Modi said. This appeal was unusual, underscoring how much the four had become instant heroes. ISRO, for its part, tightly controlled direct access to the astronauts. They held only limited press interactions, often through moderated Q&A or brief statements. Shubhanshu, being naturally reserved, navigated this new spotlight cautiously. He recognized the importance of public enthusiasm—after all, his journey was being watched by schoolchildren, inspiring future astronauts among them—but he also knew he had to keep his focus razor-sharp. As he later commented from space, 'Teamwork and support are key'—and that extended beyond his immediate crew to include the support of an understanding public giving them space to breathe.

Behind the scenes, the newfound fame added a layer of pressure to Shubhanshu's life. On quiet evenings at the training centre quarters, he would sometimes reflect on how life had changed. Previously, he could walk the streets anonymously even as a decorated pilot. Now if he stepped out, people recognized him and wanted a selfie or a handshake to 'wish him luck for Gaganyaan'. A lesser person might let this attention go to their head, but those who knew Shubhanshu observed that he remained humble and focused. 'He always had big dreams and the diligence to pursue them relentlessly,' his sister said, 'but even as a child he stood apart—disciplined and driven.' Those qualities kept him grounded. If anything, Shubhanshu became more disciplined with his routine after the public reveal—cutting down on social events and doubling down on training. Any moment not in the simulator or class, he would spend exercising or reading technical manuals, consciously avoiding the media hype swirling outside.

Yet, there were uplifting moments that came with public recognition. Schools across India began to treat him as a role model; some students even wrote letters wishing him success. ISRO arranged a few meet-and-greet sessions where the astronauts spoke to select groups of young science students. In one such closed event, Shubhanshu shared a heartfelt message: 'My journey to space will be the journey of 1.4 billion fellow Indians,' emphasizing that he felt like a vessel carrying the nation's dreams. The sense of collective pride was mutual—as launch preparations advanced, many Indians felt emotionally invested in Shubhanshu's mission, seeing in it India's arrival on the human spaceflight stage. This public energy became an invisible force propelling Shubhanshu forward. He often mentioned to colleagues how motivating it was to know that children in far-flung villages were rooting for them to succeed. It gave purpose to every tough training day.

By mid-2024, Shubhanshu had thus become both an astronaut-in-training and a national icon in the making. Balancing these roles required psychological resilience. ISRO provided media training to help the crew handle interviews and public expectations. Shubhanshu learned to answer questions about risk and fear with honesty yet optimism. In one interview, when asked if he was anxious about the dangers of spaceflight, he admitted there's always risk but expressed confidence in ISRO's preparations, saying every test and drill gave him faith that 'we will return safely'. Privately, he did feel the weight of danger—he was acutely aware that spaceflight was never routine. The 1986 *Challenger* accident and *Columbia* in 2003 were grim reminders in the back of his mind. But part of his transformation was learning to master such fears—through knowledge, through training and through a deep belief in the mission. As he moved toward the final stages before launch, Shubhanshu grew into the calm, assured leader that the situation demanded.

Bridging Two Worlds: An Astronaut of India and the ISS

Even as Shubhanshu trained for India's first crewed mission, a unique opportunity arose that would further shape his astronautic journey. In 2024, ISRO and NASA finalized a plan to send an Indian astronaut to the International Space Station (ISS) in collaboration with a private spaceflight mission. This was a bold step aimed at giving an Indian flyer real space experience before Gaganyaan, and to strengthen international cooperation. Shubhanshu was a natural candidate for this mission, given his stellar training record and leadership qualities. Thus, on top of all else, he was selected in late 2024 as prime crew for the privately-organized Axiom Space Mission 4 (Ax-4) to the ISS. Fellow gaganyatri Prashanth Nair was assigned as his backup.

For Shubhanshu, it meant shifting gears to yet another training track—this time with NASA and SpaceX. Along with Nair, he flew to the United States for specific training at NASA's Johnson Space Center in Houston. The pair spent about eight months in 2024–25 immersed in ISS systems, SpaceX Crew Dragon operations, and international crew protocols. Shubhanshu's schedule became a whirlwind—one week practising orbital manoeuvres in ISRO's Gaganyaan simulator in Bengaluru, the next week in Houston learning to operate a Dragon capsule's touchscreen displays. It was the kind of challenge he relished—essentially learning two spacecraft at once—and it solidified his reputation for quick mastery of complex systems. NASA trainers were reportedly impressed by how quickly he adapted. He already knew the fundamentals of orbital flying; now he just had to apply them to the Dragon vehicle and ISS interface. He trained under the seasoned eye of Peggy Whitson, the famed former NASA astronaut who would command the Ax-4 mission. Under her mentorship, Shubhanshu learned the quirks of living aboard the ISS: the importance of daily exercise to counter muscle loss, managing one's sleep cycle amid 16 sunrises a day, and the multicultural communication on an international crew.

The Ax-4 mission itself launched on 25 June 2025 atop a SpaceX Falcon 9 rocket from Kennedy Space Center, and it was a spectacular success. Sitting in the Dragon capsule on launch morning, dressed in SpaceX's sleek white spacesuit, Shubhanshu experienced the roaring thrust that he'd only simulated before. As the G-forces pressed him back, he drew on that centrifuge training from Russia—*this* was the real thing it had prepared him for. Within hours, he was docking at the ISS, becoming the first ISRO astronaut to board the orbiting laboratory and the second Indian citizen ever in space (after Rakesh Sharma in 1984). During the welcome ceremony on ISS, Commander Whitson presented Shubhanshu with an astronaut pin, officially recognizing him as the 634th human to reach space. It was a poignant moment—India's *gaganyatri* was now among the stars for real, decades after Sharma's Soviet-led flight. The mission was slated for about two weeks but actually lasted 20 days in orbit, during which Shubhanshu carried out around 60 experiments, including at least seven designed by ISRO for microgravity research.

Up on the ISS, Shubhanshu's transformation reached

its apex. He was no longer just training to be an astronaut—he *was* an astronaut, floating in microgravity, working alongside international peers. In a message beamed live to Earth from the ISS's cupola window, Shubhanshu addressed his countrymen in Hindi, voice brimming with emotion:

> Namaskar, my dear countrymen! What a ride! We are back in space once again after 41 years. It's an amazing ride. We are orbiting Earth at 7.5 km per second. The Tiranga (Indian flag) on my shoulder tells me that I am with all of you. This journey of mine is not a beginning to the International Space Station but to India's Human Space Programme. I want all of you to be part of this journey... Together, let's initiate India's Human Space Programme. Jai Hind! Jai Bharat!

This stirring message, broadcast on 28 June 2025, brought tears of pride to many back home. It encapsulated how Shubhanshu saw his role—as a pioneer lighting the way for India's future in space. On board the ISS he also engaged in educational outreach, holding ham-radio Q&A sessions with Indian school students—telling them, 'Many of you can become future astronauts, even walk on the Moon,' as he answered their curious questions. He spoke about how all his training in India, Russia and the U.S. had prepared him for handling emergencies in space, stressing that adaptability and teamwork were crucial lessons learned. Through these interactions, one could sense the inner transformation Shubhanshu had undergone—from a focused test pilot to a confident, inspiring space ambassador for his country.

When Shubhanshu safely returned to Earth on 15 July 2025 (splashing down near San Diego, as planned), celebrations erupted across India. The Prime Minister and President personally congratulated him for 'India's leap into commercial human spaceflight', as one analysis called the mission. There was praise for how this experience would benefit the upcoming Gaganyaan mission—Shubhanshu had effectively served as the trailblazer, gaining first-hand experience that could be fed back into Gaganyaan preparations. Some sceptics had questioned the hefty cost (reportedly around $65 million for the seat, borne by India), but ISRO defended it by citing the tremendous value of training and international cooperation derived. Indeed, Shubhanshu returned with a trove of lessons: he had lived the routine of space—the quirks of eating 'gajar ka halwa' (carrot dessert) in zero-G, the importance of securing every object lest it float away, and the need for unflappable patience when confined with others. He also saw cutting-edge ISS technology, which sparked ideas for India's own spacecraft operations. In a sense, his ISS stint was the final polish of his astronaut persona. It gave him the confidence that *yes, I can function and excel in space.* And it gave the Indian public a contemporary space hero, bridging the 41-year gap since Sharma's time.

Poised on the Edge of History

With the ISS mission behind him, Shubhanshu Shukla turned his full attention back to Gaganyaan. Now, he was not just a trainee awaiting his first spaceflight—he was a veteran spacefarer, poised to lead India's maiden crewed voyage. The latter half of 2025 found Shubhanshu rejoining his three compatriots in India, sharing with them everything he learned on the ISS. They eagerly absorbed his insights about spacecraft habitability and zero-G adjustments. Together, they ran final simulations of the Gaganyaan mission profile—launching atop the powerful LVM3 rocket, orbiting Earth at the altitude of approximately 400 km, and safely returning for splashdown in the Indian Ocean. ISRO scheduled a series of full dress rehearsals. In one such rehearsal, Shubhanshu and the crew donned their orange pressure suits, climbed into a mock-up capsule on the launchpad, and practised a launch countdown sequence. Sitting in the commander's seat (reports hinted Shubhanshu would likely serve as mission commander or pilot), he felt a familiar flutter of adrenaline. Except this time, the launch pad was Satish Dhawan Space Centre in Sriharikota, and the rocket beneath him was *India's own*. The realization was profound: all his training—from Russian forests to Texan simulators to the very vacuum of space—had led to this threshold.

Shubhanshu's family, who had coped with both pride and anxiety during his ISS trip, steeled themselves again for the upcoming indigenous launch. His mother admitted to reporters that while she was *'deeply anxious'*, she took pride in her son carrying the nation's dreams. His father's trust was unshaken: 'When Shubhanshu decides to do something, he puts in all his hard work and dedication,' the elder Shukla said. They knew he was as prepared as any human could be. In the final weeks, Shubhanshu stayed largely in quarantine with the crew, to avoid any illness and to focus their minds. Through brief phone calls, he reassured his parents and sisters that he was feeling confident and eager. Privately, on the eve of the launch, he spent a quiet moment reflecting on his journey. The boy who once bicycled to an exam in secret was now a 39-year-old astronaut about to make history. He thought of the small model aircraft he used to play with as a child and how he used to tell his sisters of his dream to fly. Could he ever have imagined flying *this high?*

On launch day, the mood was electric. As the sun rose over the coastal spaceport, Shubhanshu Shukla stood at the foot of the towering rocket, helmet in hand. A nation held its breath watching him. He exchanged a final salute with officials and flashed a thumbs-up for the cameras—a gesture of confidence. Inside, butterflies danced in his stomach, but he kept his expression steady. Every step up the launch gantry ladder, he mentally checked off the training moments that brought him here: Centrifuge—check. Simulators—check. Survival training—check. ISS mission—check. He could almost hear the voices of all his instructors, from Bengaluru to Houston, wishing him well.

Strapped into his seat in the crew module, Shubhanshu looked around at his crewmates and gave a reassuring nod. The hatch closed. Outside, the countdown clock ticked into the final hold. He tightened his grip on the armrests and took a deep breath, recalling his own words: 'Your chest, too, should swell with pride,' he had told India from orbit. Today, his own heart swelled with pride and anticipation. This was it—the culmination of the astronaut transformation, the dawn of India's new era in space. T-minus 10... 9... 8... The roar of the engines was imminent, the thrill indescribable. Everything slowed in his mind, a crystal-clear focus taking over. 3... 2... 1...

Shubhanshu Shukla's journey to the launch pad had been long and arduous, filled with trials most could only imagine. But as the final seconds ticked away, he felt ready—*truly ready*—to become what he had trained so hard to be—a gaganyatri carrying the spirit of a billion people into the heavens. And in the silent instant before ignition, he allowed himself the smallest of smiles, knowing that the next chapter of this adventure—launch—was about to begin...and with it, the moment India had dreamed of for decades.

4

Touching the Heavens—Launch, Docking and Life Aboard ISS

Liftoff: 25 June 2025—06:31 UTC

On a cool Florida morning, the SpaceX Falcon 9 rocket thundered to life at Launch Complex 39A of Kennedy Space Center. Inside the Crew Dragon capsule *Grace* sat Captain Shubhanshu Shukla alongside three fellow astronauts, ready to ride the fire into orbit. At 06:31:52 UTC on 25 June 2025, the Falcon 9 lifted off, propelling India's dreams skyward along with its multinational crew. This moment marked Shukla's ascent into history as the first Indian astronaut ever to reach the International Space Station (ISS)—and the first Indian in space since 1984. As the rocket's nine engines roared, observers knew this launch was more than routine: it was the dawn of a new chapter in global spaceflight, fuelled by a nation's hopes and the promise of international collaboration.

The journey to orbit was swift yet surreal. Within minutes, *Grace* was inserted into low Earth orbit, and weightlessness embraced the crew. 'You're pushed back into the seat—and then suddenly, there's silence. You're just floating in the vacuum, and it's magical,' Shukla later recounted of the moment engine cutoff arrived and microgravity took over. Once in orbit, the Crew Dragon began its 28-hour pursuit of the ISS, adjusting course through a series of autonomous thrust burns. Inside the capsule, Shukla peered out the window at the receding Earth—a blue marble getting smaller—aware that each passing hour brought him closer to the space station. Nearly 28 hours after liftoff, following careful orbital phasing and alignment, *Grace* was in position to rendezvous with its destination.

Docking: 26 June 2025—10:31 UTC

In the early hours of 26 June 2025, the Crew Dragon *Grace* approached the ISS, its nose cone open to reveal the docking mechanism as thrusters fired gentle pulses. At approximately 10:31 UTC, while the spacecraft soared high over the North Atlantic Ocean, *Grace* achieved soft capture—its docking ring latching onto the ISS's Harmony module at the space-facing (zenith) port. Moments later, at 10:45 UTC, hooks engaged for a hard capture, firmly attaching the Dragon to the station. The autonomous docking actually occurred ahead of schedule, a smooth and precise mating of vehicles that drew applause from mission control. Captain Shukla had officially arrived at the ISS, making history as the first Indian to board the orbital outpost. Inside the capsule, he took a moment to absorb the significance—he had travelled over 400 km above Earth, crossing into the hallowed halls of the ISS where only a few hundred humans had gone before.

After standard pressure equalization and safety checks, the *Grace*'s hatch was opened at about 12:40 UTC, and one by one the Ax-4 crew floated into the space station. They were met with broad smiles, cheers and outstretched arms. The seven members of Expedition 73—including NASA astronauts Nicole Ayers, Anne McClain, and Jonny Kim, JAXA astronaut Takuya Onishi, and Roscosmos cosmonauts Kirill Peskov, Sergey Ryzhikov and Alexey Zubritsky—had gathered to welcome the new arrivals. The scene was jubilant—warm hugs, handshakes and even celebratory drinks were shared as a symbolic 'cheers' to the visiting crew. Shukla's grin was unforgettable as he floated through the Harmony module's hatch; one of his new colleagues patted the Indian flag patch on his shoulder, a silent acknowledgement of the pride he carried for 1.4 billion compatriots back home. 'The moment I entered the ISS, I felt welcomed,' Shukla said. 'You guys literally opened up your doors like your house doors for us... The expectations I had were surpassed.' Indeed, after a brief welcome ceremony, the newcomers were given a safety briefing and quickly integrated into the station family, ready to begin their stint in microgravity.

Life Aboard the ISS

Life aboard the International Space Station was a whirlwind of new experiences, scientific work and zero-G adjustments for Captain Shukla. In those first days, he marvelled at the panoramic views of Earth from the station's cupola—the seven-windowed observation dome. Gazing down at India from orbit was especially moving; he remarked that India looks 'grand and bigger from space' than on any map. It was in quiet moments like these, floating 420 km above his homeland, that Shukla felt the full gravity of his journey (despite the weightlessness around him). He later shared a heartfelt message with everyone back on Earth: 'It is because of your love and blessings that I have safely reached the International Space Station[...] The Tricolour I bear on my shoulder makes me feel as though the entire country is with me.'

Adjusting to microgravity came with both wonders and challenges. In the first day or two, Shukla experienced the mild space adaptation sickness that many astronauts do—a mix of dizziness, a pounding head and a disoriented stomach as his body acclimated to weightlessness. 'It may look easy to stand here, but it is not; my head is aching. However, we will get used to it,' he assured during a live message, already adapting with each orbit. Before long, routine set in. Each 'morning' (as defined by the crew's schedule, since the station sees 16 sunrises a day) the Ax-4 astronauts woke from their sleeping pods, floated out, and joined Expedition 73 members to start work. The crews operated on Greenwich Mean Time (GMT), so Shukla oriented himself to a 24-hour cycle that ignored the day-night cycle whipping by outside the windows.

Scientific research was the heart of Shukla's mission. Over the course of about two weeks in orbit, the Ax-4 crew conducted *more than 60 experiments* across diverse fields. Many of these investigations were coordinated by ISRO and Indian institutions, representing India's first major foray into in-space research on the ISS. Shukla's schedule was packed from day one. Once the crew had settled in and microgravity acclimation was behind them, they dove into a full roster of experiments. In the Japanese Kibo module's Life Sciences Glovebox, Shukla carefully tended to cell cultures for a Myogenesis experiment, which examined how skeletal muscle cells degrade in microgravity and tested metabolic supplements to counteract muscle atrophy. He also oversaw Space Microalgae trials, observing how edible algae grow under cosmic radiation and zero-G—research aimed at future nutrient-rich foods for crews. In a small plant growth chamber, he helped sprout salad greens (the Sprouts experiment) to study crop cultivation beyond Earth. The Ax-4 team even nurtured tiny 'water bears' in an experiment aptly named Voyager Tardigrade—

studying how these hardy microorganisms survive and reproduce in space's harsh conditions. Shukla found it poetic that tardigrades, which can endure extreme environments, were along for the ride as humanity's tiny companions in exploration. Each day brought a new investigation— from cognitive tests (how working in microgravity affects mental acuity) to radiation measurements using a wearable dosimeter, to imaging Earth's surface for environmental and agricultural data. The Indian experiments in particular had Shukla's keen attention—he was the principal test operator for studies examining microbial adaptation, muscle regeneration and even how cybersecurity tablets perform in orbit. Through these activities, he felt like a bridge between the Indian scientific community and the limitless laboratory of space.

To illustrate a few key experiments Shukla worked on during Ax-4, here are some highlights:

- **Myogenesis**—Investigating skeletal muscle loss in microgravity and testing countermeasures to aid muscle regeneration. This experiment could help protect future astronauts from muscle degeneration and benefit patients on Earth with muscle-wasting illnesses.
- **Space Microalgae**—Growing nutritious microalgae under space radiation and microgravity conditions. The goal is to understand if algae can be a sustainable food source for long missions,

providing proteins and vitamins to crews.

- **Sprouts in Space**—Sprouting edible plant seeds (like fenugreek and mung beans) aboard the ISS to study how well crops can grow in orbit. Success here would be a step toward long-term life support, allowing astronauts to grow fresh food and supplement their diets.
- **Voyager Tardigrade**—Observing tardigrades (microscopic 'water bears') to see how microgravity affects their survival, reproduction and gene expression. Tardigrades are known for extreme resilience; understanding their adaptability could inform bioengineering or life-support systems.
- **Voyager Display**—Analysing human interaction with electronic touchscreens in weightlessness. Shukla participated in tests of hand-eye coordination and stress levels while using a tablet in microgravity, generating data to improve device design for spacecraft and habitats.

Beyond the lab work, outreach and international camaraderie were key parts of life in orbit. Shukla participated in over 20 outreach events during the mission. On his third day aboard, he took part in a historic video call with India's Prime Minister. Floating in Node-2 with a live camera feed, Shukla spoke with PM Narendra Modi, who appeared on a screen from Earth. Millions watched as Modi congratulated the crew and Shukla shared how proud he was to represent India. 'Sky is never the limit—

neither for you, nor me, nor for India,' Shukla told the Prime Minister and the students watching back home, in an inspirational message from orbit. The exchange highlighted the growing global collaboration in space exploration and surely ignited excitement among young Indians. Similar calls followed with leaders and audiences in Poland and Hungary. For instance, crewmate Tibor Kapu did a live video with Hungary's prime minister, and Sławosz Uznański with Polish officials, each astronaut engaging their home nation. These events underscored that Ax-4 was not just a private mission, but a people's mission for three countries that hadn't had astronauts in decades.

Day-to-day life aboard the ISS eventually found a rhythm for Shukla. Each 'evening', after long hours of science and station upkeep, he stole a few moments by the cupola windows to simply gaze at Earth—watching continents drift by under the station or the delicate dance of an aurora lighting up the atmosphere. He shared chai with his crew (prepared by rehydrating tea packets) and enjoyed occasional treats sent up in cargo, like a pouch of mango juice that reminded him of home. With permission, he unfurled a small Indian tricolour flag inside the station and pinned it next to his sleeping area, a constant reminder of the hopes and prayers riding with him. His crewmates playfully nicknamed him 'Shux', and around the galley table they exchanged cultural stories: Shukla taught them a few words of Hindi and described

Indian constellations, while in return he learned Polish tongue-twisters and sampled Hungarian spicy soup (all freeze-dried, of course). Every moment was a blend of hard work and wonder. As Shukla put it, 'It's not just a personal accomplishment—it belongs to all of us.' He understood that his presence on the ISS was paving the way for India's own human spaceflight ambitions, even as he contributed to the collective knowledge of humanity.

Those two weeks in orbit flew by faster than anyone expected. In total, Shukla and his crew would log 18 days aboard the ISS, conducting science experiments until the very last day. Their work ranged from cutting-edge cancer research led by Commander Peggy Whitson to technology demos of miniature spacecraft components. Together, the international team demonstrated what Axiom Mission 4 was truly about—the democratization of space and the power of international cooperation. All too soon, the time would come to pack up experiments and personal mementos, don spacesuits, and prepare *Grace* for the journey home. But until then, Captain Shukla savoured every sunrise, every experiment, and every floating conversation aboard the ISS—touching the heavens not just for himself, but for every dreamer who dared to believe this day would come.

5

Experiments in the Cosmic Lab

The humming air filters and softly blinking control panels of the International Space Station's laboratory module formed the backdrop to Group Captain Shubhanshu Shukla's daily routine in orbit. Over 18 days aboard the ISS, Shukla and his Axiom-4 crewmates immersed themselves in science—conducting over 60 experiments spanning medicine, agriculture, and space technology. At the heart of Shukla's mission were seven pioneering microgravity experiments from India, a suite of investigations that marked India's first science programme on the ISS. Each morning, as Earth rotated silently below, Shukla floated into the lab, ready to become not just an astronaut but also a researcher, farmer and explorer of living systems in space. The station's cramped corridors had transformed into a makeshift cosmic laboratory, where sprouting seeds, glowing microbes, tiny 'water bears', and human cells all became part of a grand scientific narrative.

Shukla gently pushed off a handrail, gliding toward the Life Sciences Glovebox in Japan's Kibo module. The bright illumination inside the sealed workspace cast a glow on his focused face as he prepared an experiment. Peggy Whitson, the veteran commander, floated nearby and gave an encouraging nod. 'All set, Shux?' she asked softly. Shukla smiled and recalled countless training sessions on Earth where he had practised these very motions in simulated weightlessness. Now, in microgravity, even simple tasks like transferring a drop of liquid or swiping a touchscreen demanded new adaptations. Yet here he was—steady hands, steady heart—ready to unlock scientific insights on behalf of Indian scientists watching from 400 km below. As he began the day's work, he felt the weight of expectation not as a burden, but as wind beneath his wings, propelling him through each procedure. This chapter chronicles Shukla's journey through those experiments—blending technical precision with human moments of wonder, challenge and inspiration.

Myogenesis: Rebuilding Muscle in Microgravity

Inside the glovebox, Shukla's gloved hands hovered around a biocell culture plate containing delicate human muscle stem cells. 'Myogenesis', the experiment was called—a study of muscle cell regeneration in microgravity. Its goal was ambitious—to understand and combat the muscle atrophy that plagues astronauts on long missions, while offering clues for treating muscle-wasting diseases on Earth. Floating next to him was a pouch labelled 'Metabolic Supplements'. These contained natural flavonoid compounds, which he would add to some cell samples to test if they could boost muscle repair in weightlessness.

Shukla's movements were methodical. First, he retrieved a tiny syringe filled with differentiation media, a nourishing solution. With utmost care, he injected the media into the wells of the BioCell plate—an action he would repeat every two days for eight days to stimulate the muscle stem cells to develop into fibre-like muscle tissue. As he injected the fluid, the droplet initially formed a perfect sphere in mid-air before he guided it into contact with the cell culture. He chuckled inwardly at how microgravity turned pipetting into a dance with liquid orbs, recalling scientist Prachi Nawkarkar's advice that 'simple tasks such as pipetting liquids require more practice and patience in microgravity.' Each drop delivered felt like a small victory.

Next came the supplements—a few drops of the flavonoid mixture added to designated wells. This was the core of the Myogenesis investigation—seeing whether these compounds could support mitochondrial function and enhance muscle regeneration. As he worked, Shukla narrated his steps for the camera recording the experiment, knowing that scientists like Dr Arvind Ramanathan of InStem Bengaluru were observing keenly from mission control. Ramanathan's team had a ground control culture running in parallel on Earth. The plan was to compare how the space-grown muscle cells fared versus Earth's gravity-bound ones once the samples returned home.

Shukla's mind wandered to a flashback—the lab at IISc (Indian Institute of Science) where he trained during his MTech. He remembered long hours learning to handle biological samples with precision, peering at cells through microscopes. That training was now his compass. 'Microgravity adds complexity, but the principles are the same,' he had told a reporter before the mission. In the glovebox, those words rang true. He felt a surge of appreciation for the scientific mentors and protocols that prepared him for this moment.

After securing the samples, Shukla took a moment to gaze at the cells through a magnifier. Tiny clusters of human muscle precursor cells were adhering to their scaffolds, looking innocuous yet holding secrets to major questions. What makes muscles weaken so dramatically in space? Can we block that process? The preliminary answers would come from analysis of these microcultures. As he carefully sealed the plate and slid it into the station's incubator, Peggy's voice came through: 'Nice work. Those cells are in good hands.' Shukla grinned.

He floated back, stretching his own arms and legs in mid-air—a physical reminder of the muscles he was trying to protect. Astronauts can lose up to 20 per cent of their muscle mass on long flights, and understanding the cellular causes is crucial. NASA's notes on Myogenesis highlighted that microgravity likely disrupts mitochondria, the powerhouses of cells, impairing muscle repair. By testing metabolic supplements on muscle stem cells, Shukla's work could lead to interventions that maintain muscle health during long missions. The implications excited him; he imagined future crew on a voyage to Mars, their bodies strong thanks to discoveries made in these very plates. He also thought of patients on Earth—perhaps someday an elderly person gaining mobility because of a treatment that stemmed from this experiment.

'One particular research I am really excited about is the stem cell research,' Shukla had shared during an in-orbit science briefing. 'We're trying to see if we can accelerate recovery or repair injury by adding supplements to stem cells. It's been great working in the glovebox on this,' he had told Axiom's chief scientist with visible enthusiasm. His voice carried the passion of a test-pilot-turned-scientist eager to push frontiers. Now, in the quiet after the intense focus, Shukla felt that excitement resonate within. He cleaned up the glovebox, tucking away tools, and allowed himself a satisfied breath. The Myogenesis experiment was proceeding as planned, and he was a step closer to unravelling the mysteries of muscle loss in space—and perhaps on Earth.

Before moving on to the next task, Shukla recorded a short video log. 'Day 8', he spoke into the camera, the Indian flag patch on his shoulder visible, 'our muscle cells are growing well. The supplements have been added. The team on ground will analyse if these helped boost regeneration. It's amazing—microgravity here mimics muscle ageing or disease on Earth, just faster. We're looking for what blocks muscle repair in space and whether our added nutrients can help unblock it. Fingers crossed for some promising data.' His tone was hopeful. In his mind's eye he could see the scientists back home—some of India's top biologists—nodding in agreement.

As he switched off the camera, Shukla felt a profound connection between the ISS lab and the labs across India that had nurtured these experiments. This was science without borders, stretching from Bengaluru to Earth orbit. Unhooking his feet from the workstation, he gently propelled himself toward the next experiment setup, ready to become a space farmer next.

Seeds of the Future: Sprouts and Space Farming

In the Unity node of the ISS, Shukla had set up a small growth chamber lined with petri dishes. Inside each dish, nestled in moist nutrient gel, were humble seeds of moong (green gram) and methi (fenugreek)—staples of Indian agriculture and cuisine. The experiment playfully nicknamed 'Space Sprouts' had a serious purpose—to examine how microgravity influences seed germination and early plant development. For India, a nation dreaming of long-term human spaceflight, growing food in space is a key stepping stone. And for Shukla, tending to these seedlings made him, as one headline put it, 'a farmer in orbit'.

He hovered before the clear petri plates, watching in awe at the delicate white tendrils unfurling from each seed. Tiny sprouts had indeed emerged, reaching in all directions unencumbered by gravity's pull. 'Moong and methi seeds sprout in space,' he jotted in his log with pride. Using a tablet, he snapped photos of the seedlings as instructed. The images would be downlinked to the scientists on the ground—Dr Ravikumar Hosamani at UAS Dharwad and Dr Sudheer Siddapureddy at IIT Dharwad, who led this project. Shukla imagined the delight in their labs when they saw the first-ever Indian-grown seedlings afloat in microgravity.

'Beautiful, aren't they?' came a voice. It was Tibor Kapu, the Hungarian astronaut, who drifted over to peek. Tibor had been conducting his own plant experiments and was an enthusiast of botany. The two astronauts observed the methi leaves—tiny, two-lobed and emerald green—pressing up against the petri lid. The moong shoots were a bit longer, pale stems curving gently. Back on Earth, these would be reaching for the sun, here, they don't know which way 'up' is. They just grow outwards, exploring. Plants sense gravity on Earth; take that away and it's like they have to rewrite their playbook. Fascinating, isn't it?

The Sprouting Seeds in Space experiment went beyond just getting these sprouts going. After letting them germinate for a set period, Shukla carefully moved the petri dishes into the ISS freezer, setting them to -80°C. This preservation step would lock in any microgravity-induced changes for detailed analysis later. Those seeds, once returned to Earth, would be thawed and cultivated over multiple generations to observe any genetic mutations, changes in associated microbes, or shifts in nutritional profile. The scientists wanted to see if spaceflight altered the seeds in ways that could produce hardier or more nutritious plants—traits that might be desirable for *both* space farming and improving crops on Earth.

Securing the freezer door marked another small step toward the future—one where missions to Mars or space stations might depend on tiny seeds for fresh food. Experiments with pepper and tomato seeds, even in microgravity, were beginning to inspire new interest back on Earth. The irony was unmistakable: learning to garden in space could one day transform how humanity gardens on Earth.

With the sprouts tucked away, Shukla turned to another set of seeds labelled 'Crop Seeds Trial'. This was a complementary experiment: exposing various food crop seeds to the space environment to test their resilience. In a separate kit, Shukla had rice, cowpea (lobia), sesame, brinjal (eggplant) and tomato seeds, all of which had been passive passengers on the ISS during the mission. Now he was to perform a simple but symbolic task—'irrigating' these seeds with water in microgravity—to observe how they absorb moisture and if any sprouting begins. He carefully injected a bit of water into each seed pouch. It was a subtle preview of how these seeds might behave when planted beyond Earth.

The objective here was forward-looking—to help develop climate-resilient plant varieties that could thrive in space and, by extension, in harsh conditions on Earth. It struck Shukla that by doing this, he was bridging two frontiers—space exploration and sustainable agriculture. Seed by seed, experiment by experiment, we're learning to extend life beyond our planet. He imagined a future greenhouse module on an Indian space station, full of floating fenugreek leaves and rice shoots feeding astronauts far from home.

Before closing up the seed work for the day, Shukla held one of the petri dishes up to a window where Earthlight filtered in. The sprout's green stood out against the blackness of space beyond. In that moment, he felt a wave of emotion—a flashback to his childhood in Uttar Pradesh, helping his parents water plants in their garden. He had never imagined he would one day be watering seeds in space. Each seedling, delicate yet full of promise, carried with it the aspirations of many back on Earth.

When later asked about these botany experiments, Shukla's face lit up in interviews. 'I am so proud that ISRO collaborated with national institutions all over the country and came up with fantastic research which I got to do on station for all the scientists,' he reflected. He felt like a gardener-scientist tending a cosmic nursery. And he emphasized the larger vision: Identifying plants with desirable traits for sustainable farming in space—a vision that could ensure that when humans venture further, we carry with us the means to grow life, to be nourished by the green of Earth even in the void of space.

Tiny Life, Big Resilience: The Tardigrade Trials

Floating in the U.S. Destiny lab, Shukla carefully retrieved a small canister from a foam-padded case. Inside were vials containing hundreds of microscopic creatures—the tardigrades. Often dubbed 'water bears' or 'moss piglets', tardigrades are tiny (about 0.5 mm) but renowned for their near-indestructibility. This particular experiment, informally called 'Voyager Tardigrade', aimed to test the survival and revival of an Indian strain of tardigrade (*Paramacrobiotus* sp. BLR) in space. Shukla recalled the briefing—these creatures could survive freezing, boiling, vacuum, high radiation, even 30 years in a freezer, and come back to life. If anything embodied raw resilience, it was the tardigrade.

He opened a vial and, under the microscope, saw them: tiny eight-legged specks clinging to a bit of moss substrate. At first glance, they were motionless—held in a dried, dormant state called a tun. The plan was to reanimate them with a few drops of water, letting them soak and awaken, then observe their behaviour and life cycle in microgravity. Shukla introduced a droplet of sterilized water into the vial. Through the scope, he watched with fascination as the water touched the tardigrades. Slowly, some of the shrivelled forms began to swell and uncurl. Tiny clawed legs extended. One creature started wiggling, then another. *They're alive!* he thought, a sense of wonder washing over him. Even Peggy and Slawosz floated over to take a peek—it's not every day you see an animal come back to life in front of your eyes.

Over the next days, Shukla monitored the tardigrades' revival, survival, and even reproduction. Using a handheld digital microscope, he captured footage of a tardigrade gently floating in the fluid, paddling its stumpy legs as if swimming in an invisible pond. Some of the tardigrades even laid eggs, which was a promising sign that they could complete a life cycle in orbit. The Indian Institute of Science (IISc) team that prepared this experiment was particularly interested in gene expression—what changes occur in the tardigrades' DNA activity under space stress, and which genes are responsible for their legendary resilience. So Shukla also periodically flash-froze a few specimens at certain intervals, preserving their RNA for later analysis back on Earth.

One evening, after finishing data collection, Shukla found himself simply watching a tardigrade tumbling gracefully in microgravity through the microscope view. He marvelled at its translucent body glowing faintly blue under the instrument's UV illumination, a trait of the BLR strain which forms a fluorescent shield against UV radiation. The tiny creature glowed like a sapphire speck against the black background. It struck him as poetic—a creature so small, yet so robust, carrying its own light to ward off the dangers of space. He imagined tardigrades as guardians of life's secrets, perhaps holding clues to protect humans too. If scientists could decode how tardigrades survive extreme dehydration, cosmic radiation, and freezing, it might inform everything from preserving food and medicines in harsh environments to improving human radioprotection.

Shukla's mind drifted to a memory of reading about Vikram Sarabhai, the father of India's space programme, who believed in the power of science for human welfare. Here was a direct link: tardigrade research in space could one day help develop novel biotechnologies on Earth. *From mossy walls in Bengaluru to the vacuum of space*, he thought. Indeed, this strain had been isolated from mossy concrete on IISc's campus, where it survived unthinkable conditions by fluorescing blue. Now it was a space traveller, representing Indian science in a form no bigger than a grain of sand.

He remembered the press mentioning how tardigrades preceded even the dinosaurs by hundreds of millions of years. *Ancient little astronauts,* he mused. If any life form could endure the rigors of space, it was them. Perhaps one day, tardigrades might hitch a ride to Mars, or further, seeding life or testing the survivability of organisms beyond Earth.

During a video call, a student from India had asked him what experiment he found coolest. Shukla smiled widely and described the 'water bear' he saw waking up in space. 'They're these microscopic animals that can survive almost anything,' he explained enthusiastically, 'freezing cold, boiling heat, vacuum, high pressure—you name it. We wanted to see how they do it up here. We even saw them glow blue! It's like science fiction, but real.' The students were mesmerized. Shukla realized that beyond the data, the tardigrades were becoming science rockstars for outreach—tangible, oddly cute proof of the wonders of astrobiology.

In his mission journal, Shukla later summarized the experiment: 'Study on the Indian strain of Tardigrades: primary objective—identify genes responsible for resilience. These 'ultimate survivors' might teach us how to endure space's extremes.' He reflected on how tardigrades surviving and reproducing in orbit was not just a win for science but a symbolic message—if a moss piglet can thrive up here, maybe one day humans can too, fortified by knowledge gleaned from these tiny titans.

As he stowed the last of the tardigrade samples, Shukla offered a silent, playful farewell to the resilient creatures. He imagined the forthcoming analyses by IISc researchers, aware that within those microscopic bodies lay answers to some of science's biggest questions. In that moment, he felt deeply honoured to serve as the caretaker of this celestial experiment.

Cyanobacteria and Microalgae: Green Lungs for Space

One morning, Shukla found himself surrounded by floating bags and vials tinted emerald and turquoise—a miniature algae farm in orbit. Microalgae and cyanobacteria were the focus of two ISRO-backed experiments aiming to harness these simple organisms for future space life-support. As he gently shook a bag of algae culture, watching the suspension of green cells swirl in microgravity, Shukla felt like he was holding a piece of Earth's primordial power. After all, cyanobacteria were among the first life forms to produce oxygen on Earth billions of years ago. Now, two strains of them were with him on the ISS, part of a study to see how they handle microgravity. Nearby, three strains of edible microalgae—including perhaps *Spirulina* or similar—were also growing in sealed pouches. Together, these experiments were like a test of 'space aquaculture'—could we farm algae in orbit to provide food, oxygen and recycling of waste?

Shukla had tended to these cultures daily. He'd clip the bags into a rack under LED lights, ensuring they got the illumination needed for photosynthesis. Every so often, he'd withdraw a small sample with a syringe and run it through a handheld analyzer to measure growth—cell counts, colour changes, oxygen output. It was delightful to witness. The algae were actively growing in space, turning light and carbon dioxide into biomass and oxygen, just as they do on Earth. He reported to the team at ICGEB Delhi that the algae were thriving. The scientists back home—who had sourced these strains from a Delhi wastewater treatment pond, Himalayan snow, and the Indian Ocean—were eager to learn if microgravity affected the algae's carbon capture and oxygen production efficiency. Over 14 days on the ISS, Shukla followed their protocol meticulously, even feeding the algae a controlled dose of CO_2 from a small cartridge to simulate what a life-support system might circulate.

At one point during the mission, Shukla initiated a secondary experiment involving cyanobacteria—simple organisms with complex potential. The task was to introduce different nutrients to two cultures and observe their behavior in microgravity. Two small vials were prepared: one fed with urea, the other with nitrate as a nitrogen source. The goal was to study how the absence of gravity might alter their growth patterns and protein expression in response to different fertilizers. Shukla carefully injected the nutrient solutions into the respective vials, then placed them into the station's centrifuge—either to simulate partial gravity or to ensure proper mixing. He observed something curious: the cells, which would normally sink, stayed eerily suspended in the fluid. Only after the gentle spin did they begin to settle—gravity, it seemed, had to be mimicked to make them behave.

Over time, he observed differences. The urea-fed cyanobacteria had a slightly different hue and growth rate than the nitrate-fed ones. Data from these tests would help gauge cellular responses and biochemical changes in the microbes. *Potentially,* he thought, *this could tell us which nutrient source is better for cultivating such organisms in space, or how spaceflight affects their metabolism.*

One afternoon aboard the ISS, while transferring an algae sample, Shukla attracted the attention of a fellow astronaut who floated by and observed the vivid green liquid with curiosity. The sample, derived from cyanobacteria such as *Spirulina*, resembled a thick, nutrient-rich suspension—something not unlike a 'space smoothie'. Spirulina, commonly marketed as a health supplement on Earth, is known for its high protein, lipid and vitamin content, making it a strong candidate for future space nutrition. The microalgae, compact yet potent, could one day serve as a reliable food source aboard long-duration missions—blended into drinks or even formed into compact snacks. In the evolving ecosystem of spaceflight, such bio-solutions may soon become more necessity than novelty.

Jokes aside, the Space Microalgae experiment was yielding serious insights. Shukla could see that microgravity sometimes made the algae form clumps differently than on Earth, perhaps due to the lack of convection. Some cells appeared larger and their genetic activity might be altered—samples were preserved to analyse gene expression and metabolic changes back on Earth. The idea was to compare these space-grown samples with control samples grown on Earth to pinpoint differences. Would microgravity stress them out, or would they adapt and even become more productive? The answer could inform how we design bioreactors for space. If algae grow well up here, they could be part of a recycling system—converting astronauts' exhaled CO_2 into oxygen, and waste into edible biomass. In other words, algae could act as the 'green lungs' and pantries of a spaceship.

As part of an onboard educational segment, a cyanobacteria experiment was showcased to illustrate its relevance to future space missions. Two strains of these tiny aquatic organisms—known for their ability to produce oxygen—were suspended in a translucent bag, appearing like a delicate emerald cloud. The experiment aimed to study how such organisms behave in microgravity, particularly whether they could sustain oxygen production and nutrient generation in space. Success in these areas could have profound implications: cyanobacteria might one day form the basis of closed-loop life-support systems, recycling air and waste aboard spacecraft. In future missions, entire walls could be transformed into glowing green panels—essentially algae farms—quietly working to support human life beyond Earth.

As he kept on experimenting, he realized that future was not far-fetched. In fact, a rudimentary version was right here in his hand. He felt a surge of fulfillment. When India's space agency decided to send these algae to ISS, it was with the aspiration of a self-sustaining Indian space station someday. The thought that Bharatiya Antariksha Station (as proposed) could use such tech made Shukla brim with pride.

The results so far were encouraging. In a call with ISRO, preliminary feedback was that algae growth rates in microgravity were comparable to Earth if provided mixing and light—a good sign. The cyanobacteria's biochemical activity under microgravity was being closely studied, and early indications suggested some differences in protein expression when using urea vs nitrate as feed. This could hint at how space conditions influence nutrient uptake and could help tailor how we feed these microbes on space missions.

On the last day of the experiment, Shukla carefully stowed all algae samples into return containers. Before sealing the final pouch, he looked at the vibrant green one more time. *These simple cells,* he reflected, *might pave the way for humans to live in space long-term.* In them lay the promise of air to breathe, water to drink (via recycling), and food to eat—a regenerative ecosystem packed in microscopic form. From a sewer in Delhi to low Earth orbit, this algae had travelled far, much like Shukla himself. And both were now part of a grander journey—to ensure humans not only survive but thrive beyond Earth.

Man and Machine: Voyager Display and the Human-Machine Interface

In the calm afternoons on the ISS, Shukla often participated in a rather futuristic test: he would don a headband of sensors and sit in front of a tablet screen, floating upright as best he could. This was the 'Voyager Display' experiment—a study of how astronauts interact with electronic displays in microgravity, and how it affects their cognitive load and stress levels. It might sound mundane compared to algae and tardigrades, but in the space age of touchscreens and tablets, it was *hugely* important. Spacecraft are increasingly relying on digital interfaces instead of physical knobs, so understanding any pitfalls of screen-use in zero G is critical.

Shukla tapped the tablet to begin a series of tasks. On screen, a dot would appear and he had to reach out and touch it as quickly and accurately as possible. Then lines of text would flash, testing his reading speed and comprehension. Sometimes, he had to use a stylus to trace shapes or operate a simulated control panel. All the while, the headband sensor (and possibly a chest strap for heart rate) recorded his physiological responses—heart rate, eye movement, blink rate, reaction time. The ISS's internal cameras also captured his body posture and head position relative to the screen, to analyse how microgravity might force him to adopt different viewing angles or cause him to drift.

One tricky part he noticed—without gravity, every action on the tablet produced an equal and opposite reaction on him. When he pressed the screen too hard, he floated back slightly. It was almost comical—using a touchscreen turned into a gentle dance of push and counter-push. In training, he had learned to stabilize himself by tucking his feet under a handrail. He did so now, and the tasks continued.

Peggy's voice came from the module doorway: 'How's the screen time, Shux?' He gave a thumbs-up, finishing a mental puzzle on the tablet. *Screen time*—that's how he often described this experiment to friends. But in truth, it was an advanced human factors study by IISc and collaborators, partnering with a company aptly named Voyager. They were measuring things like pointing accuracy, gaze fixation, rapid eye movements (saccades), and subjective workload while using screens in microgravity. If he got too absorbed or if the tasks were intensive, would he forget to anchor his body and float off? If text was oriented oddly relative to his eyes, would it tire him faster? If using the tablet made him more stressed or fatigued, how could spaceship designers mitigate that? These were the questions at play.

After completing a 20-minute task session, a log entry was recorded noting the completion of the round, with mild eye strain reported toward the end. Vital signs, including heart rate, remained within normal range. An additional observation was made regarding posture—without the pull of gravity, body orientation shifts subtly. There were instances of adjusting head angles in unfamiliar ways to read screens, a behaviour not typically required on Earth. Despite these adaptations, the microgravity environment was noted to be surprisingly comfortable for such tasks. He remembered the goal—results from this would inform the design of future spacecraft computers and gadgets to be more user-friendly for astronauts. India, planning its own crewed capsule and station, would directly benefit. In fact, Shukla thought of the Gaganyaan spacecraft in development—its control panel design could be influenced by what he was doing right now.

During one session aboard the ISS, the Polish astronaut conducted a neurotechnology experiment involving a brain-computer interface. Wearing an EEG cap, he attempted to use focused mental signals to control a cursor on a tablet—testing whether brain activity alone could trigger a digital response in microgravity. The study, part of a broader Polish scientific initiative, aimed to explore cognitive and neural adaptation in space. Although Shukla was not involved in the trial, he observed the session with interest. The experiment reportedly achieved a significant milestone: one of the earliest instances of direct brain-to-computer interaction in orbit, marking an exciting frontier in space neuroscience.

Meanwhile, Voyager Display had its own share of cool discoveries. Shukla noticed that sometimes after a long session, he felt a bit of simulator sickness—maybe because in microgravity, staring at a fixed screen while your inner ear senses floating can cause disorientation. He dutifully reported such feelings. The experiment also involved a device to track his eye movements precisely. How does microgravity affect gaze control? On Earth, our vestibular system helps coordinate eye motion; in orbit, that's altered. Preliminary findings showed astronauts might have slightly longer reaction times for screen tasks and possibly more eye strain or fatigue if interfaces aren't optimized. It was a subtle effect, but over long missions it could matter.

In simpler terms, as Shukla later explained to media: 'Voyager Display looked at whether using screens in space makes us more stressed or tired.' Designed by IISc Bengaluru, it gave insights that could shape astronaut–computer interaction. Even in the unique environment of space, monitoring screen exposure remained a concern—

underscoring the importance of ergonomics and cognitive health in microgravity. These observations were not trivial; they contributed to the ongoing development of safer, more efficient spacecraft cockpits and long-duration habitat designs.

After one particularly involved session, Shukla decided to unwind by doing a demonstration for fun—something visually captivating. Remembering a classic ISS party trick, he grabbed a water pouch and squeezed out a big floating water bubble in the air. Using a straw, he injected a bit of air and twirled the blob, showing how surface tension holds it together. Under the camera's gaze, he even inserted a coloured tablet, making the sphere fizz and sparkle. 'I've become a water bender here in the station,' he quipped, borrowing a line from his earlier media appearance. Peggy and the others laughed as they watched the orb wobble and shine. It was a light-hearted moment, but also educational—illustrating how microgravity transforms everyday physics, an outreach Shukla felt was important.

That night, as Shukla wrote his diary, he reflected on the role of technology and human adaptation. The Voyager Display experiment was less tangible than growing a plant or a tardigrade, but it was deeply connected to astronaut life. It touched on psychology, physiology, and engineering design all at once. And it symbolized something larger—India's commitment to not just participate in space missions, but also contribute knowledge for making spaceflight more livable for everyone. He remembered a media advisory noting that this experiment could guide interface design for India's future space vehicles. That made him feel part of a continuum—the tests he ran today might reflect in the spacecraft consoles Indian astronauts will use tomorrow.

In a contemplative mood, he floated by the cupola window, tablet in hand. The Earth at night sprawled below, a web of city lights. He imagined a time when an Indian space station might have a cupola of its own, and Indian astronauts would use tablets and AR displays seamlessly, products of lessons learned here. *This is how we make space home,* he thought, *by ironing out the little wrinkles in how we live and work up here.* With that comforting thought, Shukla powered down the tablet—enough screen time for one day—and went to catch some sleep, drifting into dreams of a future where man and machine danced effortlessly amid the stars.

Securing Space: A Quick Tech Test

Among the flurry of scientific activities, Shukla also took part in a brief but important technology demonstration focusing on space cybersecurity—essentially validating a secure tablet-based communication system in orbit. While not as headline-grabbing as glowing tardigrades or space-grown veggies, this test addressed a crucial aspect of modern spaceflight—keeping data and commands safe from errors and hacking even in space.

One afternoon, Shukla retrieved a specially configured tablet from the payload locker. Unlike the regular crew tablets, this one ran a secure communication app prototype developed by an Indian tech team. The goal was to see if the device could encrypt and transmit data reliably to Earth and between ISS modules without hiccups, and if cosmic radiation would upset its encryption keys or memory. He powered it on and initiated a series of encrypted telemetry transmissions—basically sending dummy data packets from the ISS to a laptop at mission control, with both ends verifying the encryption integrity.

Initially, all seemed routine. But part of the test was more intriguing: Shukla had to place the tablet in different locations around the station and even near a window, exposing it to varied radiation and signal conditions. This was to simulate how a device might fare during spacewalks or in different spacecraft. He followed the checklist—first using it in the shielded lab, then moving to the less-protected cupola. At each step, he checked a readout for any 'bit flips' or errors in the secure transmission. In space, high-energy particles can flip bits in a computer's memory—a known issue that can compromise encryption keys. The tablet's software had countermeasures: error-correcting codes and a backup key stored in hardened memory (an approach similar to ESA's CryptIC experiment earlier).

After an hour of testing, Shukla smiled at the results—no anomalies detected. The secure link remained solid.

He reported back, and the ground team was elated. Demonstrating that affordable, off-the-shelf tech could securely handle data in orbit was a win for future missions. This meant mission data, crew communications, even biomedical info could be kept private and intact on extended missions—a growing concern as more players access space. In an era when a stray malware introduced by a USB (as once happened on ISS) or a solar particle could wreak havoc on systems, validating robust cybersecurity was vital.

For Shukla, it was reassuring too. He thought of the upcoming era of spaceflight with tablets controlling spacecraft functions, astronauts teleconferencing with ground doctors, or scientific data being beamed to cloud servers. All that needed to be secure. He remembered reading about a previous ISS test where a tiny Raspberry Pi ran encryption trials to handle radiation issues. Now he had been part of a similar cutting-edge effort, adding an Indian contribution to the field of in-space data security.

In a lighthearted moment aboard the ISS, it was noted that even in space, the onboard devices demonstrated secure and independent functionality—aptly aligning with the spirit of technological self-reliance often emphasized in India's development narrative. Indeed, the subtext wasn't lost—India was flexing its tech muscles, showing it could bring unique capabilities to the table, from biology to cybersecurity.

He logged a note: 'Space Cybersecurity demo completed—secure tablet link functional in microgravity. Next step: integrate into crew operations.' The engineers would have more to analyse, but his part was done. Another box checked, another small step for making human space presence sustainable and safe.

Little did he know, these quiet tech validations would bolster confidence when, a few years later, Indian astronauts on the Gaganyaan orbital mission carried encrypted biomedical tablets, their design informed by this very test. In the broader narrative of Axiom-4, it was a subtle achievement—but one that exemplified the mission's spirit: covering all dimensions of living in space, from growing food to securing bytes.

Bridging Earth and Space: Reflections and Farewell

As the days on the ISS drew to a close, Shukla found himself in a reflective mood. The experiments were nearly complete, samples packed, data transmitted. In the quiet hours, he floated by the cupola again, gazing at the sprawling blue planet. India was down there, somewhere beneath the monsoon clouds, and he felt the weight of what this mission meant to his country. He recalled words spoken to him during a live video call with India's Prime Minister: the PM had congratulated him on carrying the aspirations of a billion people. Shukla had humbly replied that he was just the messenger; the science he conducted was the message—that India had arrived in human spaceflight with substance and purpose.

He also chatted with schoolchildren via amateur radio—part of the ISS Ham Radio outreach. One student asked what his favourite experiment was. He answered, 'Picking one is hard—they're like my children!' He then elaborated how each one contributes: muscle cells for health, algae for life support, seeds for food, tardigrades for science fiction-like resilience, displays for making our spacecraft better, and even tech demos for safer missions. The breadth of it struck him. Over 282 orbits and 12 million kilometres of travel, he had been humanity's laboratory technician in space, turning novel ideas into tangible results.

The final evening on station was emotional. The Expedition 73 crew and Axiom-4 crew gathered for a farewell ceremony. ISS Commander Takuya Onishi spoke warmly, thanking the private mission crew for their dedication. 'Your dedication to science and your profession definitely set a new standard for private astronaut missions,' Onishi said, raising a toast pouch. Shukla felt his heart swell with pride at that. When it was his turn to speak, he floated forward, the tricolour patch on his sleeve visible to all, and expressed his gratitude.

'I want to thank the Expedition crew for welcoming us and helping us every day,' he began earnestly. 'And to my team ISRO back home—thank you for developing our scientific portfolio, all the protocols, and even student outreach activities that engaged our whole nation,' he said, recalling the countless ISRO scientists who worked behind the scenes. 'Today's India is aspirational, fearless, confident and proud,' he added, echoing a sentiment he'd prepared. 'Truly, *saare jahaan se achha* (better than the entire world) describes our country.' Those words, borrowed from a famous patriotic poem, carried special weight in the space station's multinational setting. Peggy put a hand on his shoulder, and one could see Shukla's eyes grow moist.

He continued, 'The learnings from this mission will be beneficial to the Indian Human Space Programme—to Gaganyaan and beyond.' That was his conviction. Every test tube he'd handled, every seed he'd sprouted, every line of code run on a tablet—it was all feeding into a larger dream: India's own astronauts living and working in space routinely. *This mission is a bridge,* he thought, *between the ISS and India's future space station.* And he had been the one to lay some of the first planks on that bridge.

Later that night, as the station drifted silently over the dark side of Earth, Shukla floated near the cupola window, gazing at the curvature of the planet. The mission was nearing its end—eighteen days of intense work, seven key experiments and moments that would echo far beyond the confines of the ISS. At 28,000 kilometres per hour, he had conducted science with precision and care, but what stayed with him most was not the velocity—it was the quiet certainty that he was never alone. Every procedure, every sample, every data point was anchored in a larger purpose. It wasn't just about discovery; it was about connection.

He thought of the water bubble suspended like a pearl mid-air, shown to students across continents. He remembered witnessing the Polish astronaut testing brain-computer interfaces and the cheer that erupted when a crewmate noticed Indian-grown seeds beginning to sprout. And of course, that microscopic Indian tardigrade—wriggling defiantly in microgravity—became a symbol of life's resilience.

In each of those moments, the divisions of language, border and belief seemed to dissolve. Up here, science was the common tongue. Space, the shared canvas. And humanity, the only team.

Tomorrow, he would begin the journey home. But what he would bring back wasn't limited to data or biological samples—it was something far more powerful: a renewed sense of purpose and the quiet fire of knowing this mission had sparked something back on Earth. Somewhere, a young boy or girl in a small town may have looked up and whispered, 'I want to do that.'

And that, more than anything, made it all worth it. The racks were now tidied, experiment hardware stowed for return. The empty glovebox and quiet freezers stood like sentinels of completed work. He gently propelled himself to the cupola for one final nightly vigil of Earth. In the silence, he allowed himself a flashback to the boy who looked up at the stars from a Lucknow rooftop, dreaming of flying. That boy was now a man who had nurtured life in space. He whispered a thank you to the universe.

The next day, strapped into the Dragon capsule for departure, Shukla felt the rumble as the hatch closed. Through a window, he glimpsed the ISS one last time. He thought of all the investigations still running on board (over 60 of them, as he had been part of) and how he had contributed a slice of that grand endeavour. Peggy, beside him, grinned: 'Ready to go home?' He nodded. Home awaited—Earth, India, and eventually, the analysis and results of all their toil.

Splashdown off the Californian coast was textbook the next day. As Shukla emerged from the capsule (to the cheer of recovery teams and cameras), he carried with him the cherished flag of India and a secured case of experiment samples. In that case lay seeds that would be planted, cells that would be analysed, data that would be published—treasures of knowledge yielded by India's inaugural science voyage on the ISS.

The mission was over, but its scientific story was just beginning to unfold on Earth, in laboratories and classrooms across India and the world. Shukla knew he would spend months debriefing with ISRO, sharing results with researchers, and perhaps even co-authoring papers on muscle cells or algae growth. He relished the role—a test pilot who also gets to deliver the lab report.

In the coming days, accolades poured in. ISRO

declared the experiments a 'significant milestone', noting all seven were completed exactly as planned. Anil Prakash of the Satcom Industry Association said Shukla's mission 'heralds India's leap into the space-biotech frontier,' showcasing public-private partnership in research. The nation celebrated not just the safe return of its astronaut, but also the promise held by those small experiments: the promise that India would contribute clever solutions to humanity's push into space—be it growing food, staying healthy, or simply using a computer in zero-G.

Amid the fanfare, Shukla stayed humble. In an interview he said, 'I feel proud to have been a bridge between our researchers and the space station,' echoing his earlier sentiment. He highlighted how aspirational and fearless today's India is in taking on space challenges, and how the symbolism of an Indian conducting science on the ISS would inspire millions of students to pursue STEM fields.

In Shubhanshu Shukla's extraordinary journey, one cannot help but feel the immersive atmosphere of the ISS laboratory still lingering—the gentle whirr of fans, the sight of a tricolour patch drifting past an array of experiment racks, the laughter of an international crew sharing space and knowledge. It was a chapter where science took centre stage in a human story. Shukla's hands-on execution of those seven experiments, backed by the brilliance of Indian scientists, not only yielded data but also wove a narrative of hope, collaboration and progress.

As India looks ahead to its own space station and further missions, the scientific legacy of Shukla's Axiom-4 sojourn will guide the way. In microgravity, even simple experiments can reveal big insights—Shukla's experience proved that abundantly. And in doing so, it reaffirmed a fundamental truth he carried in his heart—the pursuit of science is a voyage outward to the stars and at the same time inward to the betterment of humanity. That dual journey—technical and emotional—was the essence of his chapter among the stars.

Sources: The insights and details in this chapter are drawn from mission reports and interviews, including ISRO and Axiom Space briefings on Shukla's experiments, news accounts of the Ax-4 science agenda, and Shukla's own reflections shared during and after the mission. These sources chronicle the purpose and outcomes of the seven experiments—from muscle cell cultures to microalgae growth—and capture the spirit of international collaboration and personal dedication that defined Shukla's scientific journey on the ISS.

6
Homecoming—Return to Earth and a Hero's Welcome

15 July 2025—Off the Coast of San Diego, 3.02 p.m. IST. Four orange-and-white parachutes blossomed against the pre-dawn darkness as Crew Dragon *Grace* drifted toward the Pacific. Inside the cramped capsule, Group Captain Shubhanshu 'Shux' Shukla braced himself. After a fiery re-entry and rapid deceleration from 28,000 km/h, *Grace* hit the ocean with a heavy jolt. Water sprayed the windows. For a moment, everything was still except the gentle rocking of the waves and Shukla's own racing heartbeat. Then a voice crackled in his headset: 'Dragon, splashdown confirmed. Welcome back to Earth!' He exhaled a long breath of relief and exchanged a grin with Commander Peggy Whitson across the dimly lit cabin. 'We made it,' Peggy said softly, giving a thumbs-up. Shukla smiled—home at last.

Recovery Operations Begin

Within minutes, SpaceX recovery teams sprang into action. At 3.07 p.m. IST, Peggy radioed Mission Control that the crew was 'ready for recovery'. Through *Grace*'s small porthole, Shukla glimpsed fast boats zipping toward them in the blackness, their lights cutting through sea spray. By 3.10 p.m. IST, two sleek inflatable speedboats had pulled alongside the bobbing capsule. Recovery personnel in gray jumpsuits and PPE masks leapt aboard *Grace*, securing harnesses to the spacecraft's hull. They first checked for any residual toxic fumes from the thrusters—a standard safety step—then signalled 'all clear' to the primary recovery ship *Shannon* waiting nearby. Floating in his seat, Shukla felt a thud as the crane's cables hooked on.

At 3.29 p.m. IST, the capsule was hoisted out of the water and gently lowered onto the deck of *Shannon*, SpaceX's recovery vessel. The hull's heat-scorched exterior steamed in the cool ocean air. Inside, Shukla felt the first tug of gravity—mild at first, then stronger as *Grace* settled into its cradle. 'Whoa,' he murmured, suddenly aware of the weight of his arms and legs after three weightless weeks. He hadn't felt Earth's pull since launch day, and now even his fingers felt oddly heavy. Peggy caught his eye and winked—she knew that sensation exactly.

First Breath of Earth's Air

By 3.40 p.m. IST, recovery engineers had rolled *Grace* to a secure platform on deck and swung open the side hatch. A rush of cool, salty sea air filled the cabin—Shukla inhaled deeply, savouring the first *real* breeze on his face in 18 days. A floodlight illuminated the opening. 'Welcome back!' called a SpaceX recovery lead, peering in with a broad smile. He offered a reassuring hand to the crew inside. Commander Whitson, in her white SpaceX pressure suit, was first to carefully unstrap. At 3.49 p.m. IST, Peggy slid out of the hatch on her own and stepped onto the deck with a triumphant grin. Crew members applauded and steadied her as she waved to a camera recording the moment.

Shukla was next. He shuffled forward inside the capsule, swinging his legs out the hatch. A medic reached in: 'Take it slow, we've got you.' Shukla gripped both sides of the hatch and eased himself onto the small egress slide, descending to the deck at 3.52 p.m. IST. Cameras flashed in the predawn gloom. He stood upright unsteadily—gravity was *real!* His knees buckled slightly, and two crewmen gently held his arms until he found balance. Shukla then lifted his arm in a jubilant wave. A broad smile spread across his face as he looked into the lens—the world's first glimpse of him back on Earth. On the live broadcast, his joy was palpable. India's son had returned.

One by one, mission specialists Sławosz Uznański and

Tibor Kapu followed out the hatch. The *Axiom-4* crew was home. All four astronauts stood side by side on *Shannon*'s deck, waving and flashing thumbs-up to the cameras as a cheer went up from the ship's crew. 'You did it!' someone shouted. Shukla could not stop smiling. Though his legs felt like lead and the world seemed to sway (his inner ear still thought he was floating), an immense sense of accomplishment anchored him. He had done it—he had gone to space and come back, making history for India.

Deck of the *Shannon*—Initial Checkups

Medics swiftly moved the crew to reclining seats set up on deck for immediate medical evaluations. Shukla sank into the chair, grateful—his muscles were already protesting the pull of gravity. Flight surgeons shone penlights in their eyes, checked pulses and asked routine questions: 'How are you feeling? Any dizziness or nausea?' Shukla felt a bit lightheaded and his stomach was fluttery, but he managed a thumbs-up. 'A little wobbly, but I'm okay,' he laughed. The doctors noted only mild orthostatic issues—normal for astronauts returning from even short missions. Indeed, after 18 days without gravity, Shukla and his crewmates were expected to need some help walking at first. As they sat resting, the crew removed their sleek white helmets. Shukla ran a hand through his hair, still damp with perspiration from re-entry. The cool breeze felt wonderful on his face. He closed his eyes for a moment, just listening to the soothing crash of waves against the ship. *It's real,* he thought, *I'm really back.*

As the capsule sliced through the atmosphere and touched down in the Pacific, halfway across the world in India, Asha Shukla stood with folded hands, her eyes brimming with tears. Her son had returned—not just from a mission, but from the vast unknown of space. While scientists confirmed re-entry data and rescue teams moved into action, a mother prayed, wept and gave thanks.

He had soared among the stars, and now he was safely home. 'We were afraid,' she would later say, her voice trembling with emotion, 'but today, there is only pride.' Her words echoed a universal truth—behind every astronaut in orbit stands a family on Earth, holding their breath between liftoff and landing. For her, the mission wasn't just a national milestone. It was personal. A journey measured not in kilometres, but in prayers.

Helicopter to Shore

Within an hour of splashdown, all initial checkups were done and the crew was cleared for transport. The sun was just beginning to lighten the horizon over the Pacific. Shukla gazed at the first hints of dawn and allowed himself a small chuckle—he had seen 16 sunrises *per day* aboard the ISS, but this one, coming after his return, felt uniquely special. The astronauts were helped onto a waiting helicopter on *Shannon*'s helipad for the short hop to the California coast. Strapped into a seat, Shukla watched through the window as the ship's deck grew smaller below. In the distance he could see *Grace*—the burn-scarred capsule that had carried him safely home—now secured and being tended to by technicians. He gave a silent thank you to the spacecraft, feeling a pang of gratitude and fondness for the vessel named 'Grace' that had lived up to its name.

The helicopter whisked them to a naval base near San Diego where a NASA jet waited. Although this was a private mission, NASA and Axiom had coordinated the crew's return logistics. A gentle cheer went up from a small group of NASA/Axiom staff on the tarmac as Shukla and team emerged from the helicopter. Still in their SpaceX suits, they waved and flashed smiles. One bystander draped an Indian tricolour flag across Shukla's shoulders spontaneously, and he clutched it proudly. A quick photo was snapped—Shukla grinning with the saffron-white-green flag, Peggy and the others beside him, in front of the SpaceX jet. It would become an iconic image in India.

By that afternoon (U.S. time), Shukla was flying eastward, heading from California to Houston, Texas—home of NASA's Johnson Space Center—for post-mission formalities. Strapped into a comfortable seat aboard the jet, he finally had a quiet moment to reflect. Outside the window, endless blue sky and clouds rolled by. Only 20 hours earlier, he had been orbiting 400 km above Earth; now he was cruising at 12 km altitude, on his way to reuniting with family. He leaned back and replayed the mission in his mind: the laughter with crewmates in zero-G, the awe of seeing India from the cupola window, the poignant farewell to the ISS two days ago, the plasma glow of re-entry. A lump rose in his throat as it hit him: *it's over. I'm really coming home.* He wasn't sad exactly—more overwhelmed, grateful and proud of what they'd accomplished. As the capsule gently rocked in the ocean swells, Shukla sat still, the harness pressing lightly against his chest, the weight of Earth gradually returning to his body—and to his soul. From the seat behind him came a quiet, knowing voice—seasoned, steady. A fellow astronaut offered a few soft words, the kind only those who've touched the void could truly share. He nodded silently, absorbing the moment.

He wasn't just processing the re-entry or the mission's end—but the immensity of what it all meant. The silence, the speed, the science, the solitude—each passed before his eyes like constellations of memory. And for a fleeting second, as he looked out the small, fogged-over window at the shimmering Pacific, his eyes welled up. It wasn't fatigue. It was something deeper. The quiet, overwhelming knowledge that he had left Earth...and returned changed.

Quarantine and Recovery in Houston

Late that night, their plane touched down in Houston. Though tempted to rush into the arms of waiting loved ones, protocol came first—the crew was ushered to a medical facility for a thorough check and a mandatory quarantine period. NASA doctors and ISRO's medical team conducted detailed examinations to ensure each astronaut was healthy after their space sojourn. Shukla's vitals were stable, and aside from some expected muscle stiffness and a bit of spaceflight anaemia, he was in good shape. Still, he and his crewmates would remain in semi-isolation for about a week to readapt and guard against any latent infections or 'space bugs' (the ISS is a controlled environment, but this precaution is standard).

To Shukla's delight, his wife Kamna and six-year-old son Kiash were already in Houston, waiting for him. That first reunion had to be behind a glass partition—in quarantine, immediate physical contact was restricted. But seeing their faces was everything. Kamna stood just beyond the quarantine glass, her hand gently resting against it, eyes shining with quiet relief. Beside her, little Kiash bounced with uncontainable excitement. Shukla looked at them, his heart full and his throat tight. He mirrored Kamna's gesture, placing his palm against the glass opposite hers. No words passed between them, but everything was said. The moment, fleeting and silent, was filled with warmth, pride and the ache of reunion delayed. It was this brief connection—this glimpse of home—that anchored him, giving him the strength to face the final stretch of medical protocols and debriefings.

Over the next week, Shukla underwent rehab therapy

daily. He did light exercises to rebuild muscle strength, practised walking exercises to recalibrate his balance, and consumed calcium and fluids to rehydrate and help his body adjust to gravity. 'It's like learning to walk all over again,' he joked with a physiotherapist as he wobbled through an obstacle course. Indeed, astronauts often feel like toddlers on return—their neurovestibular system needs to re-learn balance. By July 23, the quarantine ended and Shukla was fully cleared by doctors. He had lost a bit of weight and muscle tone in space, but nothing that a few weeks of normal gravity and diet wouldn't fix. Eighteen days in space was relatively short, and he counted himself lucky that he felt almost back to normal after only a week of rehab. Still, the first time he ran on a treadmill again, he laughed at how heavy each step felt. Gravity, he thought, was the strangest feeling in the world.

Holding Them Felt Like Home

The most emotional moment for Shukla came when quarantine was lifted and he could finally hold his family in his arms. In a private room at Johnson Space Center, Kamna and Kiash waited eagerly. Shukla, now dressed in a simple polo shirt and track pants, walked in and opened his arms wide. Kiash flew into his father's embrace with a squeal. Kamna wrapped them both in a hug, tears of joy flowing. 'Papa, can I touch you now? No more germs?' the boy asked innocently, remembering how he'd been kept at a distance earlier. Shukla chuckled, kissing the top of his son's head. 'No more germs. I'm all yours now,' he whispered. He closed his eyes, savouring the warmth and weight of his child and wife—a warmth no space capsule could ever replicate. Later, he would share a photo of this reunion on social media with the caption: 'Coming back to Earth and holding my family in my arms felt like home.' He wrote: 'Space flight is amazing but seeing your loved ones after a long time is equally amazing.' The post went viral, melting hearts across India. After all the high-tech heroics, it was this simple human moment that resonated most—a reminder that astronauts are also husbands, fathers, daughters and mothers. Shukla's journey, he reflected, was not just about exploring space—it was about cherishing what we have on Earth.

He also shared a poignant anecdote from quarantine: during separated visits, little Kiash had been told he couldn't hug Papa because Papa might have 'space germs'. The clever boy would ask, 'Can I wash my hands?', hoping that would let him touch his dad. 'It was challenging,' Shukla admitted of that enforced distance, even for a short time. It made him appreciate all the more the luxury of a simple hug. In interviews soon after, he urged everyone to 'find a loved one today and tell them that you love them,' because long missions taught him not to take family for granted. Coming from a man who had literally been to the stars, this advice carried special weight.

A Nation Rejoices—Media and Public Response

Even before Shukla touched land, news of his safe return was flashing across every screen in India. The splashdown had occurred around 3 p.m. IST, and many Indians watched it live via YouTube and TV broadcasts, hearts in their throats. When *Grace*'s parachutes deployed and the announcer confirmed 'splashdown', collective cheers erupted from Delhi to Lucknow to Bengaluru. In Shukla's hometown of Lucknow, neighbours had gathered at his parents' home to watch the live feed. As soon as they saw him emerge on deck, waving with that signature smile, the whole street broke into applause and loud cheers of 'Bharat Mata ki Jai!' (Victory to Mother India). Reporters captured emotional scenes: Shukla's mother, Asha Devi, burst into tears of joy, hands folded in prayer as she whispered thanks to God. His father, Shambhu Dayal Shukla, normally a stoic government servant, wiped his eyes repeatedly, overcome with pride. 'My son has safely returned, I thank God... I got emotional, after all, my son has returned after many days,' his mother said, voice quavering on camera. His sister Shuchi, watching her brother's ocean landing from afar, had tears in her eyes and a broad smile as she told reporters she couldn't wait to hug 'Bhaiyya' (brother) soon.

The Shukla family celebrated the homecoming in true Indian style—they cut a cake decorated with tiny astronaut figures and an Indian flag, feeding each other sweets the moment they saw Shubhanshu step out of the capsule. Television channels ran split-screen images: on one side, Shukla waving from the deck of *Shannon*; on the other, his parents in Lucknow distributing laddoos (sweet dumplings) to every neighbour who dropped by to congratulate them. 'It's a festival for us,' an uncle exclaimed to the press, describing the atmosphere in their neighbourhood. 'We are all over the moon,' his father Shambhu Dayal said with a proud smile, delighting in his unintended pun.

Across the nation and the world, congratulations poured in. Prime Minister Narendra Modi was among the first to hail the historic achievement. He posted a message on social media X (formerly Twitter) that quickly went viral: 'I join the nation in welcoming Group Captain Shubhanshu Shukla as he returns to Earth from his historic mission to space. As India's first astronaut to have visited the International Space Station, he has inspired a billion dreams through his dedication, courage and pioneering spirit. It marks another milestone towards our own human space flight mission—Gaganyaan.' The phrase 'inspired a billion dreams' struck a chord—it led many news headlines the next day. Indeed, Shukla instantly became a household name; children in remote villages who had never heard of the ISS now knew of 'the Indian who went to space for 3 weeks.'

Leaders across party lines and states expressed pride. The Chief Minister of Uttar Pradesh (Shukla's home state) jubilantly welcomed him. 'Your achievement is a proud symbol of courage, dedication and commitment to science. Today, every Indian, especially those from Uttar Pradesh, feels proud. India is eager to welcome you,' Yogi Adityanath posted. From West Bengal, Mamata Banerjee lauded 'a moment of national pride' and sent best wishes to Shukla and his family. Even opposition figures and international dignitaries sent messages—it was as if for one day, the usual divides vanished and everyone celebrated together. 'History has been made, and the future of Indian space exploration shines brighter than ever,' tweeted one prominent leader, calling Shukla's journey 'a golden chapter in India's space odyssey'.

News channels ran wall-to-wall coverage: 'Shukla Returns Safe, India's Space Hero Home.' They replayed the splashdown footage and that heartwarming moment of Shukla waving. Some anchors even got misty-eyed describing the significance. After all, it had been 41 years since an Indian citizen had gone to space—not since Wing Commander Rakesh Sharma's week-long Soviet mission in 1984 had India seen one of its own among the stars. Now Shukla had not only matched that feat but expanded it. He spent nearly three weeks in orbit—the longest ever by an Indian—and became the first Indian to set foot on the International Space Station.

Every newspaper the next morning splashed triumphant headlines. 'Cosmic Comeback: Shukla Splashes Down Safely,' wrote one. 'Indian Astronaut's Historic ISS Mission Ends in Triumph,' wrote another, noting how the $150-billion ISS finally hosted an Indian national.

Importantly, the media highlighted how this mission was not just a one-off stunt but a stepping stone for India's own human spaceflight programme. As the Indian Space Research Organisation (ISRO) chairman noted, 'the mission has its own importance for the country's Gaganyaan programme,' India's indigenous crewed spacecraft project. ISRO had invested about ₹550 crore (roughly $70 million) to send Shukla on this mission—a hefty price tag that initially raised some eyebrows. But the triumphant outcome and wealth of experience gained silenced most critics. In context, that cost was only approximately three per cent of India's overall human spaceflight budget, and many experts pointed out it was money well spent for the invaluable training and data gathered. Still, television debates buzzed: Was it worth it? Should India focus on its own missions rather than piggyback on commercial ones? A few commentators called the Ax-4 flight a 'joyride' for publicity. However, their voices were drowned out by the overwhelming public admiration for Shukla. Seeing the tricolour on his shoulder in the ISS and at splashdown filled Indians with pride. As one space analyst wrote, 'Shukla's ISS flight has become the most polarizing in recent times—yet the sight of him floating in zero-G doing science experiments made many naysayers converts overnight.' Indeed, any controversy was quickly eclipsed by celebration and forward-looking optimism.

Perhaps the most striking impact was on young Indians. Suddenly, space was *cool* again. At Shukla's alma mater, City Montessori School (Lucknow), the day after splashdown felt like a festival. The principal announced a special assembly to honour their 'star alumnus' whenever he'd visit. Students carried handmade posters with slogans like 'Welcome Back, Space Hero!' and 'Lucknow to ISS— Shukla Bhaiya, we salute you.' One Class 12 student declared to the press, 'I am super motivated now for a career as an astronaut. Space is going to be the latest fad among the young, all thanks to Group Captain Shukla, our illustrious senior.' Another chimed in that if Shukla could do it, they too could dream beyond the sky. In classrooms across India, science teachers set aside their regular lessons to discuss Shukla's mission—how he conducted seven Indian experiments on the ISS (from growing fenugreek and moong seeds in microgravity to studying hardy tardigrade microorganisms) that would aid future space endeavours. These stories fired up imaginations. Overnight, enrolment enquiries for astronomy clubs and aerospace engineering courses surged. ISRO reported a flood of messages from students wanting to know how to become an astronaut. Truly, Shukla's mission had 'stirred the imagination of youth' in India.

Social media in India was abuzz for days. The hashtag '#ShuklaSpaceHero' trended no. 1 on X (formerly Twitter). Thousands of memes and fan-art pieces circulated—one popular cartoon showed Shukla in his spacesuit planting the Indian flag on the ISS, with Rakesh Sharma's 1984 spacesuit ghost patting him on the back. Another viral post quipped: 'Move over Superman, India has Shubhanshu-man!' In a country where cricket and Bollywood stars often dominate public adulation, it was refreshing to see a space scientist take centre stage. As one editorial noted, 'For once, science class toppers have a hero in the limelight—an Air Force pilot-turned-astronaut who proved that Indians can reach the stars on our own terms.'

Honours and Homecoming Events

Back in India, plans were underway to give Shukla a hero's welcome once he returned from his post-mission debriefs. The Union Minister of Science & Technology Dr Jitendra Singh—who had closely followed Shukla's mission—announced that 'the next Indian astronaut will fly in an indigenous spacecraft,' underscoring that Shukla's expertise would feed directly into India's upcoming Gaganyaan mission. He revealed in an interview that Shukla's three-week ISS stay gave 'valuable insights and experience' as India prepares for Gaganyaan, slated to carry two Indian astronauts to low Earth orbit in 2027.

The next mission is going to be totally indigenous... Indian astronauts going for the first time in an Indian spaceship,' he affirmed. This statement electrified the nation—it meant that the *next* time an Indian goes to space, it will be on an Indian rocket from Indian soil, and quite possibly Shukla himself might be aboard.

In recognition of Shukla's achievement, there were growing calls to honour him with a high national award. Decades ago, Rakesh Sharma had received the Ashoka Chakra (India's highest peacetime gallantry award) for his spaceflight. It wouldn't be surprising if Shukla is similarly nominated for a Padma Shri or even an Ashoka Chakra for bringing glory to the nation. 'He has not just touched space, he has lifted India's aspirations to new heights,' said Defence Minister Rajnath Singh, calling Shukla's mission 'a proud stride for India's growing space ambitions.' The government hinted at a grand felicitation ceremony once Shukla is back on Indian soil, likely to be attended by the Prime Minister and top officials.

Indeed, Shukla's scheduled return to India was eagerly awaited. After finishing all post-flight formalities in the U.S., he was slated to fly home in August 2025. In Lucknow, local authorities discussed plans for a roadshow—a open-top vehicle parade from the airport to the city centre, so citizens could cheer for their hometown hero. ISRO officials planned a formal welcome at their headquarters in Bengaluru as well, where Shukla would meet and address the organization's scientists and engineers who had supported his mission. 'He is the toast of the nation, and his arrival here will only accentuate our happiness index,' his father quipped proudly, describing how their entire locality was rejoicing in anticipation.

Shukla remained characteristically humble amid the nationwide admiration following his mission. He viewed his role not as an individual triumph, but as a contribution to a much larger effort—one that involved countless scientists, engineers and support teams. For him, the true success of the mission lay not only in its scientific outcomes but also in its potential to inspire. If his journey could spark even a single child's dream of becoming a scientist or add momentum to India's space aspirations, then every moment spent in orbit had served its purpose. That sentiment was echoed by many. A senior teacher at Shukla's old school put it simply: 'Knowing how much this space voyage means for India and its upcoming Gaganyaan programme, the entire 70,000-strong CMS family—along with the rest of Lucknow—will give him a hero's welcome whenever he visits his birthplace.'

International Praise and the ISS Community

The international space community also celebrated the mission's success. Axiom Space, which managed the Ax-4 mission, touted it as a 'historic milestone for India, Poland, and Hungary'—the three countries that had astronauts on board. 'Over 60 experiments, 18 days, 3 new nations on ISS—Ax-4 showed how commercial space can expand access for all,' Axiom's CEO Tejpaul Bhatia said. NASA officials congratulated ISRO for 'taking this bold step' and expressed eagerness to collaborate on future missions. In an ISS tradition, the Expedition 73 crew (NASA/ESA astronauts who were on the station during Ax-4) had filmed a cute goodbye video with Shukla before he departed. They floated an Indian flag and a small plush tiger (India's national animal) in zero-G, saying 'Shubhanshu, come back soon!' The camaraderie built on ISS was evident. NASA's chief later commented that Shukla 'fit right in on the ISS as if he'd been training for years'—a testament to his preparation and professionalism. European Space Agency colleagues praised the international collaboration, noting that having an Indian, a Pole and a Hungarian fly together with an American commander was 'precisely what the ISS was designed for—uniting nations in exploration.'

Interestingly, Shukla's mission also sparked diplomatic goodwill. The Polish and Hungarian governments celebrated alongside India, since their nationals were also part of Ax-4. All three countries had last sent people to space in the 1980s; now, in 2025, they did so together. It underscored a poignant symmetry: the mission 'realized the return to human spaceflight for India, Poland, and Hungary, each nation's first mission to the ISS and first astronaut in over 40 years.' In a joint statement, the three governments hailed Ax-4 as 'a beacon of opportunity...paving the way for future missions and inspiring broader participation in the global space community.' Indeed, Shukla and his crewmates had shown that space was no longer the exclusive domain of a few superpowers—'access to space extends to all who seek to explore, discover, and innovate,' as Axiom's press release proudly declared.

Personal Reflections and Public Appearances

In the calm that followed the whirlwind of global headlines, Shukla spent a few quiet days in Houston—time that allowed the magnitude of the mission to settle in. The return to gravity was more than just physical; it marked the beginning of emotional processing. The sensation of floating, of gazing down at Earth from above, still lingered in his mind. Often, in the quiet of night, he found himself replaying those moments aboard the ISS—especially the view of India glowing softly beneath the curve of the Earth. That vantage point had changed something in him. The planet now seemed smaller, more fragile, more interconnected. He knew this wasn't just a personal journey—it was a shared triumph. And he looked forward to returning home, eager to translate that perspective into purpose.

Shukla believed deeply that the true legacy of any space mission lies not just in data collected or milestones achieved, but in the inspiration it ignites—especially among the next generation. For him, space wasn't just a destination; it was a mirror reflecting human potential. He often reflected on how, as a child, the idea of an Indian aboard the International Space Station felt like a distant dream. And yet, here he was—proof that persistence, discipline and curiosity could turn even the most improbable aspirations into reality.

To young Indians, his unspoken message was clear: dream without apology, pursue without hesitation, and believe that the cosmos, too, is within reach. For every future astronaut, engineer, or scientist watching his journey unfold, Shukla hoped to serve not just as a symbol of achievement, but as a spark igniting visions that stretched far beyond the classroom, into the stars themselves.

Inspiring Future Explorations—the Road Ahead

Shukla's mission marked the end of one chapter and the beginning of another for India's space journey. In the following weeks, he dove into debriefings with Axiom, NASA, and ISRO experts, recounting every detail of his training, flight, experiments and observations. These 'lessons learned' sessions were gold for ISRO. Through Shukla, Indian scientists gained first-hand insight into ISS operations, astronaut medical data, experiment design for microgravity, and even mundane details like space habitability and emergency protocols. It was like an express internship in human spaceflight. 'Shukla's space travel gave us a tremendous amount of experience and put India in a better position for large international collaborations,' Dr Jitendra Singh noted. Indeed, having an Indian on ISS opened doors—India could now envision having its astronauts on foreign missions more confidently, and other agencies saw India as a serious partner. As the minister put it, 'it also sends out a huge message across the globe—now India has come of age in the space sector.'

The immediate next big thing was clearly Gaganyaan—India's maiden crewed spacecraft project. Shukla, being one of the four IAF pilots originally selected for astronaut training, was naturally a top candidate for the mission. ISRO confirmed that Shukla remains part of the Gaganyaan astronaut corps. In fact, he had trained alongside the others (in Russia and India) before the Ax-4 opportunity arose. Now, with actual spaceflight experience under his belt, Shukla would likely play a pivotal role in Gaganyaan—if not as one of the crew who fly in 2027, then certainly as a mentor and backup. There is speculation in the space community that Shukla might command the first Gaganyaan mission, given his unique dual experience as test pilot and flown astronaut. Regardless of role, there's no doubt he will be deeply involved.

Beyond Gaganyaan, Shukla's mission has buoyed India's space ambitions further. Dr Jitendra Singh publicly revealed plans for an Indian space station by 2035—dubbed the 'Bharat Space Station'. He stated that Shukla's successful flight proves India's capability to participate in long-duration missions, which is a stepping stone to operating our own orbital outpost. 'We are looking forward to having a space station of our own... most likely by 2035, and we have also decided to name it the Bharat Space Station,' the minister announced. That ambitious goal, once merely a dream, now feels tangibly closer. If and when that station becomes reality, Shukla might very well be involved in its design or even be among its first inhabitants. He has expressed that one of his long-term dreams is to see an Indian flag permanently in space, not just as a visitor but on an Indian-built station. With the momentum generated by his mission, such dreams no longer seem far-fetched.

On the international front, India signalled it is open to deeper collaboration. Officials mentioned that when India builds its station, it would be open to hosting foreign astronauts and experiments. This reciprocity was a diplomatic win earned in part by Ax-4's collaborative spirit. There is also talk that India may join the Artemis Accords formally—the U.S.-led programme for returning humans to the Moon—which could open avenues for Indian astronauts to train for lunar missions in the 2030s. Shukla has cheekily evaded questions on whether he'd like to go to the Moon ('one step at a time,' he laughs), but friends know that if asked, he'd be the first to volunteer. He often says Rakesh Sharma inspired him by going to space in 1984; now he hopes 'to see an Indian walk on the Moon in my lifetime.' Perhaps he himself might be involved in that effort someday—as an advisor if not as the one taking that giant leap.

For now, Group Captain Shubhanshu Shukla appears poised to become a powerful voice for science and exploration. He has begun to share his experiences across a range of platforms—speaking at events like the Indian Science Congress and joining informal online discussions with space enthusiasts. His vivid storytelling—whether describing the sensation of floating in zero gravity or recalling the Ganges River glinting like a silver ribbon beneath the Earth's curve—has resonated with audiences across age groups. While his long-term path is still unfolding, Shukla may well emerge as one of India's most compelling advocates for space, science and the power of human potential.

Among the many honours and recognitions that followed Shukla's return, one imagined moment stands out in the collective vision of what his journey represents. It is easy to picture him someday walking into his old school in Lucknow—City Montessori School—wearing the blue flight suit adorned with mission patches. The auditorium, perhaps filled with young students brimming with awe and excitement, might erupt into cheers as he steps onto the stage. A patriotic tune could echo through the hall, and in that sea of young faces, a child might rise—wide-eyed, card in hand—to express a simple dream: to follow in his footsteps.

In such a moment, the full impact of his mission would be felt—not just as a scientific milestone, but as a spark lighting the imagination of future astronauts, engineers and thinkers. Though the scene has yet to unfold, it embodies what Shukla's voyage truly symbolizes: a torch passed from one generation to the next, guiding them not just to orbit, but perhaps one day to the Moon, Mars and beyond.

Shukla's journey marked more than a personal milestone—it symbolized a turning point in India's space narrative. Much like how Rakesh Sharma had once inspired a generation, Shubhanshu Shukla's mission now stood as a beacon for countless young Indians. The idea of becoming an astronaut, once distant and foreign, was beginning to feel tangible and national. Space was no longer something others did—it was something India was doing. And at the heart of this shift stood Shukla himself—humble, composed and quietly powerful—embodying both the spirit of a hero and the promise of a mentor for the future.

Epilogue to the Mission

In the quiet moments that follow the wave of celebration, Shukla is often drawn to the night sky. Now and then, the International Space Station appears—gliding silently overhead like a streak of memory among the stars. Watching it from Earth, he is reminded of the journey that took him there: a boy once dreaming under the skies of Lucknow, who would one day orbit the planet he used to trace with wonder.

There may still be new missions ahead—perhaps the Gaganyaan programme, perhaps another voyage into space. But even if his path never leads him beyond Earth again, the sense of fulfilment remains complete. The sky, once a dream, became a memory. And that in itself is extraordinary. This mission has shown what India can do. It has strengthened our belief that the sky is not the limit and that we are moving towards becoming a spacefaring nation. Indeed, as India prepares for its own crewed launches in the coming years, Shukla's contribution will be invaluable. He stands ready to lend his expertise—whether in spacecraft testing, crew training, or mission planning.

From a broader perspective, Shukla's return symbolized India's emergence in human spaceflight on the global stage. 'After the success of this mission and what Shubhanshu conducted in space—the first-of-its-kind indigenous experiments—it sends out a message that India today is ready to accept the challenges,' said Dr Jitendra Singh, referencing how Shukla performed numerous experiments for India aboard the ISS. The mission's scientific haul was significant: data from seven India-specific microgravity experiments have been delivered to

ISRO labs for analysis. This will inform everything from biology research for long-duration space stays to material science for spacecraft design. The experience is already feeding into better training protocols for Gaganyaan—for example, Shukla recommended changes in diet and exercise regimen based on his three-week stay to help future astronauts cope even better.

In a sense, Shukla became India's bridge to the ISS era and a catalyst for its own spacefuture. As one space historian put it, 'Shukla's mission will be remembered as the moment India ceased being a mere spectator in human spaceflight and became an active participant.' It has energized not just ISRO, but also India's burgeoning private space sector. Start-ups in Bengaluru and Chennai developing space tech have reported increased interest from investors, dubbing it India's 'moonshot moment' that is galvanizing a new wave of innovation. When Shukla visited a space tech incubator, young engineers flocked to show him their projects—smallsat designs, VR astronaut training modules, even a prototype lunar rover. He listened intently and offered advice, cognizant that his journey had, in some way, helped inspire theirs.

The splashdown of *Grace* on 15 July 2025 marked the successful completion of one mission and heralded the dawn of a new era for India's human spaceflight dreams. In the days after, Shukla captured this feeling in a line from one of his speeches: 'We went as visitors this time, but we'll return as hosts the next.' He was referring to

India's intent to have its own spacecraft and perhaps space station—a bold vision that suddenly felt within reach.

From the salt of the Pacific on his skin to the tears of joy in his mother's eyes; from the deafening applause of his countrymen to the quiet pride in his own heart—Shubhanshu Shukla's homecoming was a powerful, emotional journey in itself. This chapter of his life cemented his status as a national hero and an icon of aspiration. And as the nation and the world welcomed him back, Shukla's journey expresses the nation's voice that the real mission isn't just about one person going up and coming down; it's about what comes next for all of us.

Indeed, what comes next may well be shaped by the inspiration and knowledge born from this successful flight. As India charts its course to send Gaganyaan into orbit, build Bharat Space Station, and perhaps even venture to the Moon and beyond, Shukla's footsteps (or rather, flight path) will guide the way. His story—from splashdown to societal impact—shows that sometimes the return is as significant as the launch. Shubhanshu Shukla returned from space not just safely, but significantly—carrying with him the hopes of a nation, the spark to ignite future cosmic journeys, and the humble wisdom that no matter how far we travel, the greatest feeling is to come home to Earth, to family, and to a country united in pride.

7
Building the Bridge to Gaganyaan: Legacy, Leadership and the Next Generation

From Hero to Mentor

ISRO officials have openly acknowledged how invaluable Shukla's experience is for Gaganyaan. 'Ax-4 is one small step in orbit, but a giant leap in India's pursuit of human spaceflight and scientific discovery,' the agency noted, emphasizing that the *learning outcomes* from Shukla's mission—covering astronaut training methods, mission operations, and human-spacecraft interfaces—'cannot be measured purely in monetary terms.' In practical terms, knowledge that would have otherwise been unavailable to India (such as detailed exposure to NASA's astronaut training facilities and ISS life-support systems) is now directly feeding into Gaganyaan's preparations. Nilesh Desai, Director of ISRO's Space Applications Centre, affirmed that the 15 days Shukla spent in orbit provide 'extremely valuable' data to enhance the chances of Gaganyaan's success. From optimizing crew habitability systems to refining zero-G workflow procedures, Shukla's inputs are helping ISRO 'plan the Gaganyaan mission more effectively.'

Under Shukla's mentorship, his fellow astronaut corps members—group captains Prashanth Nair, Ajit Krishnan and Angad Pratap—are now better prepared to take on the challenges of spaceflight. All four men trained together in India and Russia, but Shukla alone has flown to space, making his guidance critical as the others gear up for their first mission. He has been debriefing his peers and trainers on subtle but crucial aspects of living and working in microgravity: maintaining muscle strength, managing crew schedules, operating ISS-grade life support hardware, and even psychological readiness for space. Former ISRO Chairman S. Somanath noted that the 'insights and experience gained by Shux [Shukla] during this mission will add immense value to Team Gaganyaan as we prepare for India's first human spaceflight.' In other words, Shukla's role is to ensure that India's first indigenous crew doesn't start from scratch—they will stand on the shoulders of his experience.

Looking ahead, India's human spaceflight timeline has been firmed up: three test missions (Gaganyaan 1, 2, 3) in 2025–26—including two uncrewed launches and one carrying a humanoid robot—will be followed by the crewed Gaganyaan-4 orbital mission in the first quarter of 2027. This ambitious schedule leaves little room for error, heightening the importance of Shukla's mentorship. The Gaganyaan-4 mission aims to send a crew of three into low-Earth orbit (approximately 400 km altitude) for up to a week, a feat that will make India only the fourth nation to independently launch humans to orbit. Every lesson learned from Shukla's time aboard SpaceX's Dragon capsule and the ISS is being scrutinized to inform these upcoming flights. For instance, his feedback has helped refine cockpit display designs and crew interfaces (through the Voyager Display experiment on Ax-4) to reduce cognitive load for astronauts in zero-G. His demonstrations of handling fluids in microgravity and managing daily routines have been translated into training modules for new astronauts, giving them a preview of what to expect in space.

Beyond technical training, Shukla's mission has injected a sense of inspiration and confidence into India's space community—a *human* element of leadership crucial for the next generation. His successful flight—the first by an Indian national in 41 years—was hailed by leaders as 'another milestone towards our own human spaceflight mission—Gaganyaan.' Upon splashdown, the Prime Minister lauded Shukla for 'inspiring a billion dreams through his dedication, courage and pioneering spirit,' underlining how one person's achievement can motivate many. Now back on home soil, Shukla frequently interacts with the public, especially students and young engineers, to share his journey from fighter pilot to astronaut. According to Space Minister Jitendra Singh, this mission's success 'marks a new era' for India and will 'inspire a new generation of Indians to pursue careers in science and space.' In his new role, Shukla embodies that inspiration on a daily basis—a hero-turned-mentor whose personal legacy will be the next wave of Indian spacefarers he helps prepare.

In summary, Group Captain Shukla's homecoming in 2025 was not an end but a beginning—the start of a mentorship era within India's astronaut programme. By leveraging his Ax-4 mission experience, he is actively 'building the bridge' between the hard-earned lessons of past space endeavours and the indigenous Gaganyaan missions on the horizon. As India moves steadily toward the 2027 crewed launch, Shukla's leadership at HSFC ensures that the legacy of knowledge from Axiom-4 is fully integrated into training the *next generation* of Indian astronauts, solidifying the nation's human spaceflight ambitions with both expertise and inspiration. In Shukla, ISRO has gained not just a space hero, but a mentor-captain to pilot Team Gaganyaan toward success.

Sources

NDTV News— *"Aiming For The Sky: When Shubhanshu Shukla Ran Away From Sister's 'Vidaai'"* (June 2025) ndtv.com

India Today— *"From UPSC and NDA to MTech in IISc: Shubhanshu Shukla's educational qualification"* (June 2025) indiatoday.in

The New Indian Express— *"Joy and pride laced with anxiety grip Shukla's family ahead of his space sojourn"* (June 2025) newindianexpress.com

The Times of India— *"Shubhanshu Shukla's journey: From secret NDA application to fighter pilot to India's first astronaut on the ISS…"* (July 2025) timesofindia.indiatimes.com

Livemint— *"How Indian astronaut's family celebrated as SpaceX Dragon splashed down"* (July 2025) livemint.com

Axiom Space— *"Astronaut Profile: Shubhanshu Shukla"* (2025) axiomspace.com

Wikipedia— *"Shubhanshu Shukla"* (latest update July 2025) en.wikipedia.org

NDTV News Desk. *"Shubhanshu Shukla Returns From Space as Dragon Splashes Down Off San Diego."* NDTV, 15 July 2025.

Chethan Kumar. *"Shux, Ax-4 exit Grace, here's how recovery happened."* The Times of India, 15 July 2025.

Press Trust of India. *"Splashdown! Shubhanshu Shukla Is Back On Earth!"* Rediff News, 15 July 2025.

Axiom Space. *"Ax-4 Crew Splashes Down Completing First Mission to the ISS for India, Poland, and Hungary."* Media Advisory, 15 July 2025

Jatan Mehta. *"Was Shukla's Axiom-4 flight to the ISS worth it for ISRO?"* Indian Space Progress, Issue #29, 15 July 2025.

Press Trust of India. "Shubhanshu Shukla readjusting to life on Earth, says his father." (via NDTV). 17 July 2025.

Press Trust of India. "Next Indian Astronaut To Fly In Indigenous Spacecraft: Union Minister." (via NDTV). 17 July 2025.

Josh Dinner. *"Private Ax-4 astronauts splash down aboard SpaceX capsule to conclude ISS mission."* Space.com, 15 July 2025.

The Times of India Live Blog. *"Shubhanshu Shukla Earth Return Live Updates."* 15 July 2025.

Rediff News. "Smiling Shubhanshu Shukla comes out of Dragon spacecraft." 15 July 2025.

Hindustan Times—"Shubhanshu Shukla returns, President hails it as a 'milestone for India'." 16 July 2025.

The Indian Express—"What Shubhanshu Shukla's Axiom-4 mission will mean for India's space ambitions." 15 July 2025.

The Times of India—"Shubhanshu Shukla returns safely, next mission: Helping Gaganyaan." 16 July 2025.

ISRO Official Update—*"Axiom-04 mission successfully concluded with return of Gaganyatri Shukla."* 15 July 2025.

ANI/Tribune—"Astronaut Shukla's space mission will boost India's Gaganyaan project." 15 July 2025.

Space & Defense (Andrew Curran)—*"India's First Crewed Space Flight Delayed to Early 2027."* 9 May 2025.